"Christians are often know̲̲ ̲̲ ̲̲ ̲̲ ̲̲han what they are for. This stance res̲ ̲ ̲ ̲ ̲ ̲ ̲ ̲ ̲ ̲sayer, out to coerce our compliance a̲ ̲ ̲ ̲ ̲ ̲ ̲ ̲ ̲ ̲k. In *The Gospel of Yes,* Mike Glenn o̲ ̲ ̲ ̲ ̲ ̲ and inspiring corrective. When we start living in the truth of God's 'yes,' it changes everything—our view of God, our view of ourselves, and our view of the world."

> —MICHAEL HYATT, chairman of Thomas Nelson Publishers,
> author of *Platform: Get Noticed in a Noisy World*

"I talk to people every day who have racked up a huge pile of debt and put their families at risk just so they can live someone else's definition of the good life. But Mike Glenn shows you God's way of living life from the 'yes.' Now you can say 'yes' to destiny, 'yes' to forgiveness, 'yes' to God!"

> —DAVE RAMSEY, *New York Times* best-selling author and nationally
> syndicated radio host

"This is not a 'prosperity gospel, name-it-and-claim-it' book. This is a 'glorious God, love Him and praise Him' book. All Christ-followers will be challenged and encouraged by it. Mike Glenn provides a solid biblical foundation for building authentic relationships with God, with others, and with ourselves."

> —SANDRA D. WILSON, PhD, seminary professor, spiritual director,
> and author of *Into Abba's Arms* and *Released from Shame*

"Mike Glenn is my pastor, friend, and counselor. He is the right person to author a book about a positive approach to the power and purpose of Jesus Christ. Mike's emphasis on changing our negative views to those things positive was evident back when I first met him. Now, in *The Gospel of Yes,* he has given all of us the 'yes' that he instilled in me."

> —BRAD PAISLEY, Grammy Award–winning recording artist
> and Country Music Association Entertainer of the Year

"Too many Christians are living a smaller life than the one God designed for them. They accept unnecessary limitations because they fail to trust God's 'yes.' When you listen to God's 'yes,' you find your identity and discover your calling. Let Mike Glenn point you toward your destiny as you hear the most powerful word God will ever speak to you."

—MARK BATTERSON, author of *The Circle Maker, Soulprint,*
and *In a Pit with a Lion on a Snowy Day*

"Mike Glenn is that rare incisive, profound thinker who knows how to put the cookies on the lower shelf where the rest of us can enjoy them. *The Gospel of Yes* is filled with chewy delights. Don't miss these treats."

—JERRY B. JENKINS, *New York Times* best-selling author and owner
of the Christian Writers Guild

"Soon after I started *The Gospel of Yes,* I was no longer reading the message; I was *savoring* the message. I heard afresh how much God loves me. I heard anew how much He cares for the plans of my life. I heard that God is more interested in telling me 'yes' than 'no.' And my reaction at the conclusion of my reading surprised me. I wanted to read it again."

—THOM S. RAINER, president and CEO of LifeWay Christian Resources

"When we want to accomplish something, we don't think about the places we *don't* want to go, just the place we have determined to reach. *The Gospel of Yes* is all about living in line with that purpose. Having watched Mike live out his 'yes' and seeing the explosive growth of his church, I am glad he took the time to share his blueprint with the rest of us."

—SKIP PRICHARD, president and CEO of Ingram Content Group

"This was one of those books where my highlighter wore out before I even finished the introduction. I can't wait to see what will happen to a culture that, up to this point, has believed that God's favorite word is 'no.' They will be changed by *The Gospel of Yes.*"

—JON ACUFF, *Wall Street Journal* best-selling author of *Quitter*
and *Stuff Christians Like*

We Have Missed the Most Important Thing About God.
Finding It Changes Everything.

THE
GOSPEL
OF
YES

MIKE GLENN

WATERBROOK
PRESS

THE GOSPEL OF YES
PUBLISHED BY WATERBROOK PRESS
12265 Oracle Boulevard, Suite 200
Colorado Springs, Colorado 80921

Details in some anecdotes and stories have been changed to protect the identities of the persons involved.

ISBN 978-0-307-73047-3
ISBN 978-0-307-73048-0 (electronic)

Cover design by Kelly L. Howard; photography by Sharon Green/Corbis

Published in the United States by WaterBrook Multnomah, an imprint of the Crown Publishing Group, a division of Random House Inc., New York.

WATERBROOK and its deer colophon are registered trademarks of Random House Inc.

Library of Congress Cataloging-in-Publication Data
Glenn, Mike.
   The gospel of yes : we have missed the most important thing about God. finding it changes everything. / Mike Glenn. — 1st ed.
      p. cm.
   Includes bibliographical references (p.   ).
   ISBN 978-0-307-73047-3— ISBN 978-0-307-73048-0 (electronic)
   1. Christian life. 2. Submissiveness—Religious aspects—Christianity. 3. Obedience—Religious aspects—Christianity. I. Title.
   BV4501.3.G59 2012
   248.4—dc23

                                    2012002014

Printed in the United States of America
2012—First Edition

10 9 8 7 6 5 4 3 2 1

To my teachers: Bill Leonard, Hardy Clemons,
Wade Rowatt, and David Garland

Because you lived your "yes," I was able to find mine.

Contents

FOREWORD

Mike Glenn, a preacher and a pastor and a writer, has taken his life of church ministry and brought it all to bear on one common word: *yes*. It's not wise to rank Bible verses, as if to suggest that one might be better than another. But allow me to suggest that near the top of my list would be 2 Corinthians 1:20: "For no matter how many promises God has made, they are 'Yes' in Christ. And so through him the 'Amen' is spoken by us to the glory of God."

This verse contains two big words: *yes* and *amen*. All the Bible's promises, every one of them, say "yes" when they see Jesus, and then all creation echoes that "yes" with a cosmos-echoing "amen!" As I read *The Gospel of Yes,* Mike made me see so many "yeses" in Christ, and I kept saying "amen." It happened on nearly every page. The "yes" followed by "amen" can be called (and I borrow an expression from my friend Margaret Feinberg) "the sacred echo of life."

Go ahead. Read the Bible, and make a list of God's promises, and then take a look at Jesus Christ. When you do that, you can say, "All those promises are a big 'yes' in Christ." The Bible's promises had been wandering for centuries, and then, from a distance, they spied the figure of a Galilean. He was a crucified Galilean who came back to life in a cosmos-shattering reversal of death. When those promises saw Jesus, they shouted throughout the land a big, hearty "yes." It seemed to come from the bowels of the earth and the heights of heaven all at the same time. When this happens, we say "amen."

Mike shows us how those promises find their way home to Jesus. When we say "yes" to God, we hear God say a big "amen." That, too, is the sacred echo of "yes."

It gets real personal too. God's "yes" in Jesus Christ leads to our discovering who God made each of us to be. Mike opens our eyes to the truth that God has said "yes" over us, and it is our simple calling to do God's "yes" and to *be* that "yes." We learn to let God's "yes" guide us, shape us, and mold us into a God-glorifying echo of what those promises discovered when they found Jesus. We learn to say "amen" when the promises find Jesus, and in saying "amen" we find the unique "yes" that God made us to be.

—Scot McKnight
Author of *The King Jesus Gospel* and *One.Life*

ACKNOWLEDGMENTS

No project like this is the work of one person. Many people had a hand in shaping the thoughts contained in the following pages. My parents, John and Barbara Glenn, raised me in a home of faith and love. My wife, Jeannie, who is always my greatest supporter, loved and encouraged me through some of my toughest days. My sons, Chris and Craig, did their best to raise their father well.

The believers who make up Brentwood Baptist Church support and encourage my ministry. Few pastors have the privilege of working with a congregation that has the commitment and abilities that the people of our church have. I love being your pastor and friend. To the young men and women who make Kairos, thank you. I have learned so much from you. To the staff of BBC, you do great work and allowed me the time to write this book. Diane Mayfield, my administrative assistant, kept me on time and focused...well, as much as she could. Mark Sweeney, my literary agent, made sure somebody besides the two of us knew about the book. Ron Lee and the WaterBrook team have made this a much better book, and I am grateful for their efforts. Any flaws that remain are totally mine.

I offer this book to anyone who will read it, and I pray that Christ may use it to open lives to the "yes" of living "for," which we can find only in him.

Our Desperate Need to Hear God's "Yes"

For God did not send his Son into the world to condemn
the world, but to save the world through him.

—JOHN 3:17

The lesson that changed my life came out of a crisis. I had been the
pastor of my current church for slightly more than a year when I
learned a longtime staff member was having an affair. The affair had
been going on for nearly three years, but none of us knew about it.

When the news began to leak out, some people in the church questioned if my leadership could be trusted in such a critical matter. I hadn't
been on board long enough to earn their confidence. What's more, I didn't
know whom I could trust. Who had the ear of the doubters? Whose advice should I listen to? While I didn't have all the answers, I did know
that one way or another, the church and I would get through this. We
had no other choice.

And we did get through it. The church stayed together, and by the
grace of God, both families affected by the affair stayed intact. By the
time the church began to recover, however, I was coming close to losing
it. I was wrung out, drained dry, beyond exhaustion. There was nothing
left inside me.

I cried. I cried a lot. I prayed a lot. I told God how angry I was at the way things had gone. How could a trusted member of the pastoral staff have done something like that? Some of the church's members would never get over it. Innocent families were still trying to work through the pain of betrayal and humiliation. Because of the actions of two people, a church and its future ministry were now in doubt.

I wasn't the only one who was angry. People were angry at me, as well as the minister involved and the person with whom he had the affair. I was one of the few people who knew all the details. What one person hadn't told me, somebody else had. Sometimes knowing things you don't want to know about other people is an exhausting burden. This was not the way I had seen my ministry working out, but this was the way it was going.

Sometimes God Shows Up

Still drained and running on empty, I had to prepare for a planning week with the pastoral staff. Leading up to it, I got away to my parents' house on a lake in north Alabama to pray and work through the plan. As I spread my resource materials across a large table in the kitchen, it hit me that I might not be around to preach the sermons I was about to plan for the coming year. Too much had happened at the church, and when you work through a crisis like this one, sometimes you become a daily reminder of the pain everyone has suffered. Like Moses, some pastors can get you to the River Jordan but not into the Promised Land. Maybe God had brought me to this church to get everyone through the crisis, but now, having gotten them through it, I would have to be replaced by someone else who could lead the church into its future.

I can't tell you how betrayed I felt. I had thought I was coming to a creative and energetic congregation where I had a chance to make a real difference. Now that dream was being buried in the rubble of lies and betrayal. My anger kept burning. Why should my ministry end prematurely because I had to protect innocent people from the details of all that had happened?

Everything I had been holding inside for months erupted at the lake house. I came apart. I prayed, but if you had been there, you might not have called it prayer. You would have called it screaming. God had betrayed me. He had kept things from me. Why didn't he warn me in advance what things were like? Why did he send me there, knowing I'd walk into a firestorm of someone else's making?

I demanded answers. I really wanted God to come there, to the lake house, and put up an honest fight. I was ready to exhaust myself wrestling with God, just as Jacob had.[1] I'd hang in there all night if I had to, and I was willing to walk away with a limp if that was what it took. At that moment, in light of what I was facing back at my church, the limp seemed as if it would be sweet relief.

But God did not come.

The next morning I sat in a rocking chair on the back porch. God hadn't answered, and I told him I couldn't go on like this. I made it known that I wasn't leaving the chair until something changed. I didn't whisper that prayer out of boldness or even great faith. It was nothing that noble. Either something would change, or I would give in to complete despair.

I sat on the porch all day.

At dusk suddenly the air felt different. I can't explain it other than to say I knew God was coming, and he was coming close. Just as suddenly, I was terrified. The God I had been so bold with in demanding that he show up was now approaching. What was I going to do? I was afraid he would blow me off the planet. While moments before I had been defiant in my refusal to move, now I was too scared to move. I found myself holding my breath and bracing for whatever was next.

In the silence I heard two sentences. The first was "Why don't you let the church relax and be who I made her to be?" The second was "Why don't you relax and be who I made you to be?" That was it. As fast as the moment had come, it was over.

I began to cry again. Other than the first moment when I knew I was forgiven and accepted by God, when I was seven years old, I had never heard more liberating words. How simple. How profound. How consistent with all that I knew about God and his love for me. If God had indeed created me, then why didn't I trust how God intended to use me? Doesn't it make sense that with God, the Ultimate Designer, form and function would be totally aligned?

I returned to Tennessee to the staff meeting where we planned the sermon schedule. God had asked me why I didn't just relax and be who he made me to be and why I would try to do anything other than let the church be who he created her to be. I took his words to heart and began talking about how God had created us to work together in ministry.

Our congregation is unique in a lot of ways. We would never be comfortable following fads or trends, no matter how successful they might be somewhere else. The people who had been drawn to our church already knew who God had called us to be. The church had heard its "yes" from God.

Now I needed to ask myself some questions:

"Why me?"

"Why here?"

"Why now?"

Who had God created me to be? Honestly, I didn't know. I had just endured the most horrendous year of my life, leading a congregation of hurting people through the aftermath of a leader's sexual infidelity. Why had I been required to suffer the brunt of the reaction to all that?

God knew, and he had given me the freedom to relax and be who he made me to be. I am a firstborn, type A perfectionist. In years past, success for me involved making everyone happy. I lived to please my parents, my teachers, and the people in my congregations. I thrived on those moments when I surpassed the expectations I perceived others had placed on me. It's no wonder I reached a point of desperation after the crisis.

I was leading others, but I had never thought through my own life. I had never discovered who I was and did not understand the purpose for which I was created. I knew God had a plan for me. But oddly enough, it had not occurred to me that God had created me as a person whose gifts and temperament are in line with his purpose for me. I'd always thought God would grab me, ill suited as I was, and start hammering me into whatever plan he had decided on.

This next thing will sound strange, and as I write this, I admit that I regret it took me so long to gain this insight. It had never occurred to me that God might want me to enjoy my life! How could I have missed that truth?

I'd always been taught to be suspicious if things got too easy or if I felt too happy. Feeling good was suspect, and feeling bad was thought to be evidence that a person was faithfully following God. And I was far from being the only one who believed this. A friend told me that he thought at one time he was supposed to be in the ministry. He felt God's will had been confirmed when—and these are his exact words—"I was sufficiently miserable."

Sufficiently miserable. Why do Christians think God would spend time making plans for them that are guaranteed to ruin their lives? Stating it like that makes it sound absurd, I know. But it captures my former assumptions about God and about life. The idea that I might actually *like* the plan God had for my life had never crossed my mind.

THE JOURNEY OF "YES"

After reaching a point of desperation and demanding that God show up and provide some direction, my eyes were opened. God wanted me to relax. He wanted me to be me, using gifts he had given me. He wanted me to concentrate on doing things I was good at, things that utilized the best of who I was. He wanted me to enjoy my life and my work for him. So I began to pay attention to the way I was wired. What was I created to do, and what had I been trying to do for which I had no real talent or gifts?

Paul reminds us in 1 Corinthians 12 that every believer has been given gifts to serve the body of Christ. He also reminds us that no one person has all the gifts. This way the members of the body learn to synchronize their abilities in the synergy of the Spirit. This was true for me as well. I had some of the gifts but not all of them. So what did that mean for me and for the congregation I led?

I was affirmed in preaching and teaching. I was affirmed in seeing where our church should be going and how we should best respond to changing opportunities. In pastoral care I was passable, but I lacked the clinical training to do much beyond traditional caring ministries. And as for administration, well, I was horrible. One of my friends (and he still is my friend) turned to me in a meeting and said, "Mike, you not only don't help the church when you attend administrative meetings; you hurt the church." Yes, that observation stung, but I knew it was true.

We began to rework my job description so I could spend more time doing what I do best. Sure, that process was painful, but in the end it was joyously liberating. Remember, God wants us to relax and be who he made us to be. He wants us to enjoy what we do.

The next thing I did was resign from all the civic groups I had joined. It's great to be involved in local service organizations, but that doesn't mean you have to serve on committees or go to all the meetings. I am not good at meetings. I lack the time, and, honestly, I lack the patience. That's not right or wrong; it's just me. Since I resigned from the civic groups, everyone is happier. I am, and so are the people who used to be in meetings with me.

Upon first hearing this idea, you might think that finding and living in your "yes" would be limiting, even constricting. Nothing could be further from the truth. In fact, it has been the most liberating experience of my life. I am free to throw my full energy into the things I am gifted to do—and without any guilt or hesitation. I don't waste time trying to get better at things I'm not good at. And it no longer bothers me to say, "I'm really not good at that. Someone else should do it." I am free to be who I was created to be, and I am comfortable with the limits God has lined out for me. Garrison Keillor, in his book *Lake Wobegon Days,* says it this way:

> Some luck lies in not getting what you thought you wanted but getting what you have, which once you have got it you may be smart enough to see is what you would have wanted had you known.[2]

He's right, you know. Once you find the "yes" of God, you discover it's the very thing you would have wanted if only you had been smart enough to ask for it. Fortunately, we don't have to look hard to find it. God is eager to show us, but we do need to ask.

1

Does God Have a Favorite Word?

The good news could rightly be called "the gospel of yes"

"How do you know me?" Nathanael asked. Jesus answered, "I saw you while you were still under the fig tree before Philip called you." Then Nathanael declared, "Rabbi, you are the Son of God; you are the king of Israel." Jesus said, "You believe because I told you I saw you under the fig tree. You will see greater things than that."

—JOHN 1:48–50

If you're serving Jesus, it's not supposed to be about happiness, right? The goal of submitting to Christ is not to assure your own sense of satisfaction.

That's true, as far as the statement goes. Serving God *is* about faithfulness and obedience, not about seeking personal happiness. But serving God and others in ways you were created and gifted for brings a natural sense of joy and soul satisfaction. These feelings come from the synergy of your life connected to God's Spirit and involved in a realm of Kingdom missions work that you were designed and equipped for. These things come to you from living within God's plan and design.

But if this is true, why are so many Christians convinced that if they aren't miserable, they must have drifted outside God's will? My best guess is that we were taught this from an early age in church. Or at least we were taught things that led us to reach this conclusion.

Think about it. We knew we were sinners, and we lived in fear of God's judgment. The object was to avoid hell, and we were willing to be miserable on earth if that improved our chances of gaining an eternal reward. Yes, we heard about God's grace and love, but the amazing truth of that reality didn't sink in. What did come through and leave a lasting impression was communicated between the lines: "Whatever you do, don't do anything wrong." Your experience might be similar to mine. I attended a church where I was told what *not* to do. Not doing things took on a sheen of righteousness. My friends and I would get together on Sunday and praise God that we hadn't done anything all week. We were convinced that scrupulous inactivity was what God preferred.

Beyond that, we were schooled on what we opposed. We were against dancing, drinking, cursing, smoking, and several other things I must have blocked out of my memory. I don't take self-destructive behavior lightly, and I don't endorse sin. God did not design us to do things that would destroy us. Yet following Jesus is much more than being careful not to do wrong. When you look at Jesus's life and study what guided him, it had nothing to do with following rules or meeting anyone's expectations. From the start he kept moving forward to accomplish his mission. He came to earth to seek and to save that which was lost,[1] and every day he took steps in that direction. He overcame sin for all of us, and never once did he accept avoidance as an appropriate action.

A Christian is one who follows Christ, and based on the example he set, we know that following him involves much more than just being against sin and anything else we find objectionable. Living against things is far too limiting. Defining your life by what you oppose makes your life small, and it can fuel anger and bitterness. But Christ showed us a different way. He opposed sin and evil once and for all. But notice how he did it. He sacrificed himself and offered his life, which was his "yes" to the Father's will as the solution to the problem of sin. The "yes" of Jesus, even to the point of death, was the only thing that could conquer sin.

Jesus was not "attacking the opposition" as most Christians understand that phrase today. Instead, he moved steadily toward the cross because he understood that was where his "yes" was taking him. Saying "yes" in obedience to the cross also meant saying "yes" to the life of the resurrection—for himself and all who would follow. There is no greater joy and soul satisfaction than this.

The Bible teaches us to "overcome evil with good."[2] Jesus's life shows us how to win people, not how to pound them into submission. Jesus is the perfect example of a life lived *for*, not against. We are called to live for Christ, not against the world. Yes, following Christ often will place us in conflict with the world. But such conflict is not something we originate; it is a natural consequence of following Jesus. The biblical directive for all Christians is to follow Christ, not just to oppose the world.

You can't live a life of substance by living against.

Serving the God of "Yes"

I got my first hint of this truth when I was struck by a verse in the Sermon on the Mount. "All you need to say is simply 'Yes' or 'No'; anything beyond this comes from the evil one."[3] If you grew up attending church, as I did, you know that this was the proof text most often cited to forbid cursing. Christians were not to invoke anything other than their honest intention to follow through on what they said they would do. We were to live in such a way that our word was indeed our bond. Casual use of the Lord's name was not tolerated. Say "yes" or say "no."

I was a kid when I first heard this verse, and I understood that using bad language was wrong. But I also thought that saying only "yes" and "no" would be pretty boring. Plus, was anything beyond "yes" and "no" *really* demonic? That seemed to go a little overboard to me. Why would Jesus issue such an extreme warning?

I had to be missing something. Sometimes reading one of Jesus's teachings is like looking at a body of water. Just by looking at the surface, you can tell a lot. Rivers and lakes, ponds and oceans all look different. But you will never know how deep the water is until you wade into it. The same is true with Jesus's teachings. You read them and say, "I know what that means." But if you sit with them, holding his words in your mind and heart, the words will reveal an entirely new depth. The words of Matthew 5:37 are a good example of this. Simply let your word "yes" be "yes," and your "no" be "no."

This verse is about integrity. *Integrity* means "trustworthiness" or "consistency." A steel beam has integrity when it can be trusted to hold up a roof even when the roof is blanketed by two feet of heavy, wet snow or is pounded by gale-force winds. In the same way, our lives have integrity when our values, decisions, words, and actions hold up under pressure.

Circumstances will change, but the character of people of integrity doesn't change. They live their "yes" in Christ—who they are in him. Every other decision flows from these essential wellsprings of the soul. Jesus confirmed this in the gospel of Matthew: "But seek first the kingdom of God and His righteousness, and all these things shall be added to you."[4]

THE GOSPEL OF "YES"

When you accept the "yes" of Christ's redemptive grace and respond with the "yes" of faith, everything finds its rightful place. Your life finds order, meaning, and the right fit in your community. Finally you can relax in who God created you to be.

If a decision before you doesn't serve your "yes" in Christ, then the response is "no." You throw it out. Looked at in this light, your "yes" is indeed "yes," and your "no" is "no." Anything other than that is out of bounds. Since only your "yes" in Christ serves your purpose in life, anything else is not of God. It is demonic.

In Philippians, Paul wrote of his longing to know Christ and nothing else:

> But whatever were gains to me I now consider loss for the sake
> of Christ. What is more, I consider everything a loss because
> of the surpassing worth of knowing Christ Jesus my Lord, for
> whose sake I have lost all things. I consider them garbage, that
> I may gain Christ and be found in him, not having a righteous-
> ness of my own that comes from the law, but that which is
> through faith in Christ—the righteousness that comes from
> God on the basis of faith.[5]

For Paul, the only thing that mattered was to know Christ. Everything else—even his own life—he considered disposable. "I will let everything else go," Paul said, "if I can just get a tighter grip on Jesus." This is the yes-and-no focus of life that I believe Jesus was pointing to. Paul got it. Few of us do.

Paul brought up two important points. First, he knew what he was *for*. He was for getting as close to Jesus as he could. That was his all-consuming vision. Paul had said "yes" to Christ as fully as he knew how, and that meant everything else was a "no."

Contrast that with the way most Christians live today. They can't tell you what they are for. But they can describe in great detail what they oppose. Paul took the opposite approach. He introduced much of the known world to the gospel, an achievement made possible because of a powerful positive vision. He wasn't waging war against the pagan religions that held sway in the Roman Empire. He was taking the "yes" of God to people who were needy and unaware of God.

Fear and anger are sometimes necessary motivators (get out of the burning building!), but they can't inspire a person for a lifetime. Fear turns to despair (nothing matters anyway; we'll never get out alive). Anger turns to bitterness (the whole world is against me). But a vision that pulls us toward a positive and meaningful future can sustain us through all kinds of hardships. Athletes push themselves beyond their physical limits and musicians practice uncounted hours in the single-minded pursuit of the elusive moment of perfection. The same principle applies to each of us, however pedestrian our lives may seem. If we understand who we are created to be in Christ, we realize we have an all-consuming calling. Our calling—our "yes" in Christ—is what focuses our lives and determines how we invest our lives.

THE FOCUS OF "YES"

If you know your "yes," then you can simply let go of all the things that don't help you get closer to Christ. I suppose we'll always need sermons that warn listeners about the dangers of the world. Yet I'm convinced most of us need something far more effective: a consuming vision of Christ that centers our lives and drives us in a positive way. Sermons would accomplish much more, I believe, if they stirred our imagination and fired our passion with God's "yes."

I know there are objections to this idea. I hear them often whenever I suggest a focus on "yes":

- But isn't this too tight a focus? So tight it limits our lives?
- Doesn't doing what you are suggesting cut us off from all kinds of options and possibilities?
- Wouldn't we be likely to overlook what needs to be corrected because all we can see is what you're calling "yes"?
- Don't you think we need to be warned of the dangers of the world so we'll know what to avoid?

Is God's "yes" too limiting? How could it be? It defines our purpose, our shape, and what we are best suited for in life. Asking God to focus your life is liberating. Here's an example. As I write this, my wife, Jeannie, and I have just celebrated our thirty-first wedding anniversary. We've been together a long time, and let me be very clear: I do not feel deprived. I found my "yes" in Jeannie, and from that moment on, any possibilities related to some other romance were "no." Knowing your "yes" rescues you from untold hours of wavering back and forth over the countless options life uses to distract you. It's true we have far more options than any other generation. But most of the choices we are offered are irrelevant to our happiness. Does it matter what color your shirt is or whether your shoes are in style? Getting to know your "yes" allows you to ask one simple question of everything that comes along: does it help me get where I am going? If it does, then choose it. If not, then drop it.

What makes life increasingly difficult is to know what you are against without knowing what you are for. Being against divorce doesn't make you *for* marriage. Being against poverty doesn't necessarily mean you're going to help the poor. Knowing what you are against doesn't mean you have the energy or conviction to drive toward a positive goal.

And this brings us to Paul's second point: It's not enough to live against. You have to live *for*! But saying it and living it are two different things. Start living for all the things you believe in, and you'll find the world does everything it can to shift your focus back to a negative setting. Negative pronouncements are used in political campaigns, fund-raising efforts (send in money to help us defeat the bad guys), and religious disputes (it's common to demonize those who hear God differently). The fact is, it's easier to tear down than to build, to point out a problem rather than come up with a solution.

Honestly, living against things requires less effort. You can point out a problem, criticize it, and feel as though you've done your duty. But when you say "yes," you bring with it the willingness to take initiative, to be creative, to apply your gifts and abilities to positive, proactive solutions. Most people assume that choosing "yes" will limit your life. It's just the opposite. Choosing "yes" opens your life to all kinds of possibilities, including unexpected breakthroughs and adventures.

No Limits

Jeannie and I have two sons. As they grew older, we learned that they felt completely free to pick up a phone and call us at any time. And even at home, when they were too young to be out running around with friends, they would invade our lives whenever the thought struck them. They are grown now and on their own, but we are still their parents and always will be. That's just the way it is.

There are similarities between the life of a parent and the life of "yes." Both lives are focused, available, and without limits. When artists say "yes" to their craft, they know that perfecting their skills will demand countless hours in the studio or seated with the instrument. Great artists are gifted individuals, but they pay a very high price. In his book *Outliers: The Story of Success,* Malcolm Gladwell says that it takes about ten thousand hours of work in a discipline to be considered an expert.[6] You can find that level of commitment only in "yes."

Our world is phobic about commitment. We go to extraordinary lengths to avoid being pinned down. Couples live together without being married because they are afraid of the commitment. Church membership is down, but attendance is up. Why? People will go to a church, but they won't join. Memberships of all kinds are down—book clubs, bowling leagues—all because people have a growing wariness of commitment. People don't want to be put in a situation where others can ask them to do something that might prove difficult or even just inconvenient.

This avoidance extends to hesitation regarding a sold-out relationship with God. There are lots of things that might cause reluctance. For one, God might ask too much of us. He might demand that we give and give until we give ourselves away. Yes, you do give and give because, as Jesus taught, "For whoever wants to save their life will lose it, but whoever loses their life for me will save it."[7] Giving your life away is the only way to save it.

When Peter complained that he and the other disciples had left every-

thing to follow Jesus, Jesus replied that in the coming age whatever anyone had forsaken for the cause of Christ would be paid back one hundred
times.[8] Committing yourself to the "yes" of Christ isn't losing everything
but letting go of anything that competes with our loyalty to him. In exchange you receive the good and eternal things Christ desires to give you.
It's in dying that you live and in giving that you receive. I know it sounds
backward, but, in reality, saying "no" to everything but your "yes" in
Christ gives you clarity and energy, the way focused light makes a laser.
Saying "yes" allows you to focus on what matters.

Preaching "Yes"

A few years ago my church decided to start a Tuesday-night worship
service for young adults.[9] We called it Kairos, the Greek word for "time."
We have an extended worship period, an unhurried time of prayer, and
then I teach. There is nothing unusual or dramatic about the service, and
yet it has become one of the best things I do. I love Kairos because of the
relationship I have with thousands of young adults.

I have been surprised by how eager young adults are to talk to someone about their lives. While the worship services usually last about an
hour and a half, the after-service conversations often last longer. I can't get
over how willing people are to wait when it means they can have a deep
conversation. For some, their stories have to be told. Someone has to hear
about their journey. For others, confession has to be spoken. And others
are looking for insight to clear up the confusion they feel.

Sometimes they begin by telling me how bad they feel about a decision they made. They feel trapped by the consequences of past choices
and don't see a future for themselves. Others are confused by the myriad
choices available to them. People can become paralyzed when they face
too many options. Choices about jobs, graduate school, and careers are
difficult to make when you also are facing the questions of how to pay
this month's rent or why your girlfriend hasn't called in a week.

No matter what the challenge or struggle, I ask the same question: "Tell me about your 'yes.'" People who just the moment before were struggling with the complexity and difficulty of a situation they are facing suddenly will stop and think. Often their faces wrinkle in concentration. For many, the question about "yes" is perplexing. It's one they had never thought about.

"What do you mean?" they will ask.

"What's your 'yes'?" I will say again. "Jesus said, 'Let your yes be yes,' so what is your 'yes'? If you know your 'yes,' then all the 'nos' will take care of themselves. So have you found your 'yes'?"

Life will run you ragged, and if you don't find the right focus for your life, just sorting through all the choices and decisions will exhaust you. So here are four basic questions you need to ask and answer:

- Who am I?
- Why am I here?
- Do I have a purpose, and if so, how do I find it?
- Is there meaning in life, or is all of this just some kind of cosmic crapshoot?

When I talk about how God created the universe for the purpose of relationships and how each of us is part of the delight that the Father has in his creation, that captures their attention. What if, as the story of Adam tells us, we were created to be stewards of God's universe? If that's true, then each of us has a role to play in the Divine Plan. Each of us is uniquely gifted and wired to be in relationship with God, and part of that relationship is working with him to redeem—to pull back—a portion of the universe that has been lost to sin. Sure, I know this will be finished only when Christ returns, but God is always working to reclaim his creation. He will not cede one bit of it to the powers of darkness. That means his people are always aligned with and working to fulfill his mission.

When people grasp this idea, the wheels in their heads begin to spin another way. Suddenly a new world opens up with the asking of one question: "What if?"

- What if I really am created in the image of God, and what if that reality has a special meaning for me that is different from other people?
- What if God did create me on purpose, *for* a purpose?
- What if I am the way I am, not because of a random combination of genetic material, but to fill a particular need and role in God's plan?
- What if we could find a way to understand the reason for which we were born?

Then the questions begin to pop up right and left:

- Okay, then what was I made for?
- If God put me together in a particular way, then what do I naturally like and what don't I like?
- When am I the happiest—doing what and investing myself in what way?
- Could the answers be clues to the question of how to live, how to direct my life?

Athletes talk about being in the zone. The zone is a state of concentration, an alignment of emotional, mental, and physical abilities where the game seems to slow down and the play becomes almost effortless. I believe we were called to live more in the zone than out of it. Being aligned with God's Spirit, riding the Divine Current, makes whatever we are doing more impactful, more elegant, and more joyful.

Paul made this point to the Christians in Colossae when he wrote, "And whatever you do, whether in word or deed, do it all in the name of the Lord Jesus, giving thanks to God the Father through him."[10] In this statement Paul ordained work as an act of worship. Whether we are planting crops, paving a road, teaching a class, or filing documents, we should do everything as if we were doing it for Jesus himself. One of the things we lost in the Fall—meaningful work—Jesus has restored in the gospel.

When you understand your life's "yes," you can focus on what matters in and for your life. Being able to say "yes" to God's "yes" in you means you already have answered the majority of life's most important questions. With these answers confirmed by God's Spirit in the deepest places of your soul, you can move forward with confidence and power.

I believe God wants us to live in that zone, experiencing a lifetime of moments where identity, destiny, and opportunity come together in a resounding "yes" of meaning and joy. This book is about finding your "yes"—and having the guts to live it.

2

The Problem of Living with "No"

*You were created to live **for**, not against*

> So I was afraid and went out and hid your gold in the ground. See, here is what belongs to you.
>
> —MATTHEW 25:25

Have you ever wondered why the first word most toddlers seem to learn and use, repeatedly, is *no*? It's probably because that is the word they hear most often. When they open a cabinet door or pull the dog's ears or run too fast down the hall, the word they hear is *no*. For good reason, I guess. Without hearing *no* and hearing it a lot, most toddlers would get into dangerous situations.

So it's easy for parents to develop a habit of saying *no*. No matter what a toddler wants to do or what he asks for, the easiest, quickest, and safest answer is *no*. Parents get used to saying it, and toddlers get used to hearing it. Then one day the toddler learns to say it, and he keeps on saying it long after becoming an adult. One generation after another has been trapped in the habit of *no*.

Don't get me wrong. *No* is a necessary word. In fact, it's an integral part of any true *yes*. The word *decide* comes from a Latin root meaning "cut away." To say *yes* to one thing requires that you say *no* to other things. Every *yes* carries with it a *no,* and *no* defines our limits as created beings. There are things we cannot do. God, in his mercy, gives us limits for our own good. There are things in the world that are dangerous, and like any good parent, God says "no" to us. But the "no" of God is also positive. Like the banks of a river, our given limits increase our power by focusing our potential.

WHAT IS GOD SO AGAINST, ANYWAY?

It's easy to see how we grow up assuming that God's word to us is always "no." If you conducted an informal survey asking people about their views of the Christian God, they would say, "God is against a lot of things. He says 'no' a lot." But as we discussed in chapter 1, that's a faulty assumption.

In the beginning God gave Adam and Eve nearly free rein of the garden. They could go anywhere they wanted and drink anything they wanted, but they couldn't eat fruit from one tree in the overflowing, luxuriant garden! That hardly makes God a hateful tyrant, intent on killing our fun. But once we conclude that God is against things, that "no" is his favorite word, we apply the same mistaken thinking to the rest of life. We assume that because God says "no" to a few things, he has forbidden everything.

Even the Ten Commandments, which are written mostly with a negative tone, are outstanding examples of God's "yes." Still, bring up the Ten Commandments, and while no one will remember all ten, everyone will know "Thou shalt not!" (You have to say this phrase from the original King James in a deep and serious tone to get the full effect.) The commandments are much more than that, but for some reason the negative imperative is all we remember.

God Opposes Just Ten Things

God didn't say "no" to everything, just to ten things. "Now that you are free from slavery and living as my people, here are ten things you can't do." And what are the ten? Let's look at them.

And God spoke all these words, saying:

"I am the LORD your God, who brought you out of the land of Egypt, out of the house of bondage.

"You shall have no other gods before Me.

"You shall not make for yourself a carved image—any likeness of anything that is in heaven above, or that is in the earth beneath, or that is in the water under the earth; you shall not bow down to them nor serve them. For I, the LORD your God, am a jealous God, visiting the iniquity of the fathers upon the children to the third and fourth generations of those who hate Me, but showing mercy to thousands, to those who love Me and keep My commandments.

"You shall not take the name of the LORD your God in vain, for the LORD will not hold him guiltless who takes His name in vain.

"Remember the Sabbath day, to keep it holy. Six days you shall labor and do all your work, but the seventh day is the Sabbath of the LORD your God. In it you shall do no work: you, nor your son, nor your daughter, nor your male servant, nor your female servant, nor your cattle, nor your stranger who is within your gates. For in six days the LORD made the heavens and the earth, the sea, and all that is in them, and rested the seventh day. Therefore the LORD blessed the Sabbath day and hallowed it.

"Honor your father and your mother, that your days may

be long upon the land which the LORD your God is giving
you.

"You shall not murder.

"You shall not commit adultery.

"You shall not steal.

"You shall not bear false witness against your neighbor.

"You shall not covet your neighbor's house; you shall not
covet your neighbor's wife, nor his male servant, nor his female
servant, nor his ox, nor his donkey, nor anything that is your
neighbor's."[1]

So let's get this straight. God is against murder, stealing, lying, adultery, and being jealous of what your neighbor has. Is anyone *for* these things? Honoring one's parents is the commandment that is stated entirely as a positive, the implication being that God opposes the dishonoring of parents. But isn't showing honor to your parents a good thing? And keeping the Sabbath involves taking a day for rest and reflection, which is good for your health and well-being—emotional, physical, spiritual. Secular thinkers and writers who are concerned about human productivity in our 24/7 world are counseling people to take a day off and unplug from their gadgets. Spend a day in quiet and rest, and reconnect with core values. This is what God told us to do. How is that a bad thing?

When you look at things God opposes in light of how damaging they can be, the commandments take on an entirely new power, even beauty. Let me show you what I mean. The first commandment tells us not to have any other gods before God. There are those who say God's ego demands this kind of singular attention, but it has nothing to do with divine ego and everything to do with connecting humans with the one and only true God. "There is no other god like me, and I alone have the gravitational weight to hold everything that is in you in its proper orbit. If you put anything or anyone in the place that is reserved only for me, your life will spin out of control." Could it be that the first commandment is given to us in mercy, to keep us whole, to position us in right relationship with the only God who is God?

In the second commandment God says, "Don't make any images of me." What if God is saying to us, "I am not a God you can understand or fully comprehend. I can be known only by encounter"? Again, isn't this commandment an invitation of grace? The God of the universe is inviting us into a personal encounter with him. How can that be a bad thing?

And the others? Who better than God can know exactly what is best for you, what you need most? We are limited in understanding, but God has no limits. You've heard the saying "Be careful what you ask for, because you just might get it." We are shortsighted, and we never see the complete picture. Many of us find we are thankful, after the fact, that God chose not to answer certain prayers. When God tells us "no," he has good reason to do so.

The Ten Commandments, those great "Thou shalt nots," are gifts of grace and mercy. God offers them to us as guardrails for a positive way to live—the *best* way to live.

THE GREAT COMMANDMENTS

When Jesus was asked which commandment was the greatest, he answered by putting two commandments together. In the gospel of Matthew, he pulled the Ten Commandments down to two: " 'Love the Lord your God with all your heart and with all your soul and with all your mind.' This is the first and greatest commandment. And the second is like it: 'Love your neighbor as yourself.' All the Law and the Prophets hang on these two commandments."[2] I find it interesting that Jesus stated the Great Commandments in a positive manner.

According to him, if we follow these two commandments, we have been obedient to all ten of the original commandments. When we have loved God with everything we have and are and have loved our neighbors as we love ourselves, we have found a way to keep the other commandments as well. Loving God and being loved by God allows us to love others with a depth that isn't possible on our own. In the same way, being loved by God and loving God in return allows us to understand and, therefore, to love ourselves in ways we can't do by ourselves. Only with God's presence in our lives through his Spirit are we able to authentically keep these commandments in both the letter and spirit of Jesus's teaching. Neglect one aspect of these two commandments, and they all fall.

One more thing: when your mind and heart are focused on the positive aspects of loving God and loving your neighbors, you won't allow a lot of space for the negativity of sin in your life. Loving others is hard and can't be done on your own. It keeps driving you back to God. And when you are driven back to God, you are filled with his peace and become better able to love yourself. At the same time, when you know you are loved by God, you are better able to love your neighbors without manipulation or games.

MORE THAN SIN

Jesus said he came that we might "have life, and have it to the full."[3] Yet, because most churches focus so much on sin, our lives as believers rarely focus on life, much less its fullness. For too many of us, Christianity has been narrowed down to sin management. Sure, we all want to go to heaven. But under the sin-management paradigm, getting to heaven is no longer about Jesus's sacrifice on our behalf and his invitation to follow him in a new life. The focus on sin makes getting to heaven a matter of keeping score. You get points for doing good things and lose points for doing bad things. Being a Christian becomes a spiritual frequent-flier program. If you work at it hard enough and accumulate enough points, you can fly for free.

I know all about this scoring system, because it describes my early spiritual experience. Keeping up with all those points is exhausting. A good week is a week when you don't lose any points. When I was young, adding points was a definite plus, but the main thing was not to lose any. And you could lose points for all kinds of things: using bad language, not going to church, watching the wrong movie, or doing anything else that might reflect badly on your Christian witness. That last category was particularly problematic because it was so subjective. You could be doing something good, such as helping a friend work on his car. But because the friend had a bad reputation, you could be accused of hanging around the wrong crowd and *lose* points!

Somehow, following Jesus stopped being about, well, following Jesus. It was all about getting and keeping points. My friends and I discovered there were enough low-risk ways to earn points, such as church attendance, that we didn't need to do other good things if they involved any risk. For instance, we didn't follow Jesus into places or friendships if they could backfire on us and cause us to lose points.

"He's a good boy. He never does anything wrong." We would hear this at church. But the adults never said anything about Christians— young or old—who were out there doing anything right. Because doing nothing wrong was valued, my friends and I measured success in things *not* done.

THE DAMAGE OF NEGATIVE THINKING

Simply not doing wrong isn't enough. Being against sin isn't the same as being for Christ. Yes, we walk away from sin to follow Christ but not until we have said "yes" to him. We say "no" to everything else, not to earn brownie points or to look good in someone else's eyes, but because we want to know Christ. If all you think about is not sinning, then sin takes center stage in your thinking. As James warns us in the first chapter of his letter, what we think about becomes what we do, and what we do becomes who we are.

I have a confession to make. I love Oreo cookies. For me, nothing is better than a new bag of Oreos and a glass of ice-cold milk. Now that's a party! I also like to maintain a nominally healthy weight. These two desires are mutually exclusive. I can't maintain a healthy weight and eat all the Oreos I want. So what do I do? I firmly resolve I will not eat *any* Oreos. By doing that, I have placed an Oreo in the center of my mind. For the rest of the day, I think about how I will not eat an Oreo. In fact, I think about it in ravenous detail. *I will not,* I tell myself, *eat an Oreo by twisting it in half and licking the filling off first, then dunking the chocolate part into ice-cold milk. No, I will not do that.* After expending all sorts of mental energy to deny myself a cookie and, as a result, being preoccupied all day by a cookie, I go ahead and have one. And after eating one, I might as well eat them all. I feel guilty of course. I have failed. And I resolve never to eat another Oreo…and the cycle starts all over again.

As long as our first thought is *What do I need to avoid?*, the guiding influence in our lives is sin, not Christ. To be sure, we are working hard to avoid things that God disapproves of, but we are missing God in the process. The hard work of avoiding a mistake or misstep looms so large that God gets blocked from our view. If all we think about is sin, even when we're thinking of ways to avoid it, we increase our chance of failure. This is the irony of sin-management Christianity.

Instead, as Paul taught, fill your mind with Christ and let go of the rest. Sin and the desire to sin will be pushed out of your life the way light chases darkness from a room. If you live for the "yes" of Christ, the "no" of sin will gradually cease to be a major issue.

Paul wrote in Philippians, "Finally, brothers and sisters, whatever is true, whatever is noble, whatever is right, whatever is pure, whatever is lovely, whatever is admirable—if anything is excellent or praiseworthy—think about such things."[4] Paul, in encouraging the young church at Philippi, gives us a brilliant insight into the essence of following Christ. When you fill your mind with good and beautiful things, those images and thoughts are revealed in your behavior. So study Christ in the Scriptures, memorize his teachings, meditate on his miracles. Focus your thinking on Jesus, and the rest of your life will follow.

This, of course, is why we have to be careful about what we allow into our minds. Images from our media-driven culture—television, movies, pictures in magazines, attachments sent to us in e-mails—have a way of sliding into our brains and staying there. And once we see these images, we can't unsee them. And when they stick, they soon become our thoughts, and our thoughts become our actions. This, of course, is what makes pornography so dangerous. What we see in pornography soon becomes what we do.

But if we fill our minds with the things and thoughts of Christ through worship, Bible study, and prayer, his presence continues to expand in us until his life fills ours. Again, to quote Paul, we should strive to have "Christ in you, the hope of glory."[5] Christ in us, transforming us into his likeness from the inside out. The things in us that don't conform to his image are pushed out and discarded. His "yes" defeats the "no" within us.

COUNTING SALVATION

If living to avoid sin is so problematic, why are we quick to adopt that pattern? One reason is that it is much easier to keep score. Baseball fans enjoy filling in a scorecard during a game. Hits, runs, errors, changes in pitchers—it can all be captured on a card, inning by inning.

A similar dynamic is at work when a Christian focuses on avoiding sin. Are you growing and maturing as a believer? How can you tell? "Growing and maturing" sound so vague. It's hard to know when you're making real progress, so you start keeping score. You keep a mental chart that plots sin avoidance. If you work really hard at not messing up, the scorecard can make you look pretty impressive.

Let's face it, we prefer things we can quantify, count, and cut into percentages. Living out the gospel in a positive way is hard to count and harder to prove. What do you have to show for it? It's much easier to count all the times you avoided sin in the past week. Plus, avoiding sin keeps things simpler and makes dealing with people much easier. If someone you know messes up, you can find a reason not to help her deal with the consequences. She made her bed, so she can lie in it.

When you live in service to "no," it's easy to conclude that offering compassion to a sinner is to condone the sin. If someone's life falls apart due to a broken marriage or actions taken under the influence of alcohol, you can tell yourself you are under no obligation to help. The person crossed the line, and now he has to pay the price.

And we all know that hanging out with a drinker or a divorced person might tempt you to drink or consider straying from your own marriage. And even if you are not tempted, your being seen with the "wrong crowd" will raise suspicions at church. Sure, Jesus spent a lot of his time with known sinners, but he was the Son of God. Most of us aren't that strong. Better just to say "no" and keep saying "no." If you risk saying "yes," it could cause you to lose points.

We are trained to live as slaves to "no." How does the verse of the old hymn go? "Would he devote that sacred head for such a worm as I?"[6] Worm? God looks at me and sees a worm? If I wasn't feeling bad enough about myself already, I am now. (Modern hymn translators felt so bad about the word they changed "a worm" to "sinner.") Being told how worthless I am—a mere night crawler that does its best work when impaled on a fishhook and tossed into a pond—never helps. But some people don't feel as though they have been in church unless they leave feeling unworthy of God's love. I know; I was that person.

And if you're unworthy of God's love, for sure you are not made of the stuff it takes to plunge into a life of following Jesus. Walk with Jesus and you know what will happen: you'll be exposed to risks and temptations, because he'll take you to risky places. It's so much easier to avoid all that by simply saying "no."

THE WORLD OF "NO"

The church taught us we're worms, and the world does its part by telling us about all the things we are *not*. This is why I hate going to the grocery store. The problem is the checkout line, specifically the magazines in the rack hanging just above the conveyer belt. Week after week I see the same thing. There's a list of the ten most beautiful people in the world. I am not on that list. There is another list of the ten richest people in the world. I am not on that list either. I am not on the list of best dressed or most talented, best hair, best smile, best…well, you get the idea.

By the time I get through the checkout line, I feel like the biggest loser in the world. (Yeah, there is a list for that as well, and I didn't make that one either.) In a matter of seconds, my soul has been pounded with a two-by-four of negative realities. I have been told repeatedly about all that I am *not*. What's more, I have been told I will never get there. I slink out of the store, knowing I need to do something to get what the world says I don't have. And this, of course, is where the world wants me.

Once you are convinced you are lacking, you have to buy something to make up for it. Our nation's economy is based on consumers buying stuff. To help feed the economy, marketers exert intense pressure on us to buy more stuff. They create discontent by constantly reminding us of all the things we are *not*. Then they promise, falsely, that when we buy their product or service, we will overcome our deficiencies.

Of course, being reminded of what we are not can work in the opposite fashion as well. It can elevate our self-image because we compare ourselves with those we consider our inferiors. Let me show you how. Reality shows are the most popular shows on television. They come in various forms: men and women in "real life" situations, unknown artists looking for their big breaks, families dealing with tough situations. People are put in a high-pressure situation and left there, with their lives on display for our entertainment. We gather around the television like the crowds in the Roman Colosseum, waiting for another contestant to crash and burn.

The next day we stand around the coffee urn at work and talk about the poor souls whose lives we saw disintegrating on network television. We feel better about ourselves because we are not the singer who forgot the song lyrics or the drunk driver who was arrested on *Cops*. We may be messed up, but thank God we are not like those crazy housewives living in New Jersey. We gather at church on Sunday and shake our heads over how painful it must be for the pregnant teenager whose tragic life was featured on a television talk show, then we head off to Bible class.

Most of us don't know the "yes" of who we are; we only know what we are not. This is a sad way to live, a long way from the "yes" that God offers us in Jesus Christ.

FROZEN IN FEAR

Living "against" leads to the worst kind of despair. Sooner or later you begin to understand that even if you avoided every sin, it would never really change anything. It wouldn't change who you are. When you wear yourself out doing all you can do, it still isn't enough. This is where I think most Christians live. They have found a place of tolerable misery (if it feels bad, it must be God's will) and have settled in for the duration. They don't expect much from their relationship with Christ. Most are just trying to mind their own business and keep a low profile until they can get to heaven.

This is the fear that keeps most Christians from engaging in the adventure of life. Adventures lead to dilemmas and quandaries that have no simple, easy answers. *Yes* and *no* lie at opposite ends of the continuum, and there is a lot of space in between where most of life takes place. Deciding in advance that you always have to land firmly in one or the other, either fully yes or completely no, locks you into an untenable position. If you pursue a yes/no life, you will tend to retreat from much that you encounter every day and thus avoid the struggle of living out your faith. Or you might choose to duck behind a theological bumper-sticker slogan that is designed to shut off any further conversation or thought. Either way, you feel that you are avoiding sin and keeping clear of making a mistake.

That might be the safest approach, but it's not the Christian life. If you don't risk failure, you won't learn much about holy living, serving others, and obeying Christ. Insisting on such a yes/no life leads to a spiritual dead end if your first desire is to live faithfully as a follower of Jesus.

I understand why following Christ is unsettling to most Christians. They are convinced that God is keeping accounts, and every time they slip up—even when they are seeking to minister to others—God will write it down. "Jeff put himself in the path of temptation when he joined his neighbor at a barbecue where there was foul language, women in immodest outfits, and drinking." If every failure is held against us for eternity, we're in trouble. And that mistaken belief weighs heavily on Christians.

But it's not true. We have already been washed clean by Christ's blood. Yes, we are to resist temptation. That much is clear. But nowhere in the Bible does it suggest that we will always succeed and will never mess up. It is impossible for us to finish life with an unblemished record, but that's no reason not to try. We do fall down, but we keep getting up. As the apostle Paul said to the Philippians, we "press on."[7] So we don't need to waste our lives attempting to pull off the impossible.

The greater sin by far is not to try, to avoid opportunities to get involved in people's lives, to refuse to use our talents in helping others and in showing them the love of God. Things that need to be made right aren't made right simply because someone who was supposed to try didn't. We are the ones Jesus put there to help or, at the very least, to try to help.

Saying "no" makes our lives smaller. I understand why we feel that "no" seems to fit us. We realize we are failures. Everything we see and hear reminds us of how flawed we are. And after years of living this way, we grow comfortable in our lack of effort. We give up on our dreams. Life becomes survival. We might do a pretty good job of avoiding what's wrong, but we don't do anything right.

In the gospel of Matthew, Jesus tells the famous parable of the talents. The master in the story entrusts three servants to oversee part of his wealth while he is away. When the master returns, he finds two servants have done well and doubled what he had entrusted to them. The third servant, afraid of the master's anger, buried the talent given to him and simply returns it unused and with no increase.[8] The master is furious but not for the reasons we assume. He is not angry because the servant tried and failed or because the principal had produced no greater value. No, the master is angry because the servant simply *didn't try*.

Sadly, most Christians are that servant. They have locked away any potential of engaging the world for a Kingdom purpose because they are afraid of what God will do if they fail. This is a tragic misreading of God's character and the work of Christ on the cross. We don't understand how much God loves us, how much his mercy has already covered and will continue to cover, and how perfect and complete Christ's sacrifice is for us. And because we believe a lie, we never understand that the greater sin is not to try at all.

We have concluded that avoiding hell is more important than following Christ in any practical, daily, risky way. So we shut ourselves off from the world and the God who created it. This is why the gospel of Jesus Christ is such a shock to many Christians. We assumed Jesus would come to earth and say "no." We never expected him to preach "yes." But his message should not come as a surprise. He came, he said, to preach the message of his Father, and his Father has been saying "yes" all along. The champions of our faith—Abraham, David, Mary, and all the rest—are simply those who heard and believed the "yes" of God in Jesus. They heard the same "yes" that God spoke to call creation itself to life.

And we are invited to hear that same "yes" today.

The "Yes" of Creation

From the start, God's approach
to us has been "yes"

God saw all that he had made, and it was very good. And
there was evening, and there was morning—the sixth day.

—GENESIS 1:31

I was in my front yard with a bunch of friends from the neighborhood. We were standing around my science-kit telescope, trying not to move too much, not even to breathe too hard. We were whispering to one another as if we were afraid that by speaking too loudly, we would lose the magic of the moment.

This was a big night because we had found Saturn. After what seemed like hours of moving my telescope a millimeter at a time, we had locked in on the ringed planet. And we were looking at it, all the way from my front yard across 796 million miles of space (at its closest point). It was hard to believe. We were looking at Saturn!

We eagerly took our turns, careful not to touch the telescope while trying to get our eyes as close as we could to the cold metal eyepiece. (In Alabama, winter is the best time to sky gaze.) The satellite *Cassini* took almost seven years to reach Saturn in 2004. I felt a little smug when I heard NASA's announcement. I had already seen the planet when I was a kid.

I've never forgotten that moment. The wonder of it, the beauty that makes you hold your breath in awe, afraid that any movement will ruin the magic. We all have had such moments—walking on a beach watching a storm roll in, staring into the glowing orange red of a summer sundown, standing on a mountain where you feel as if you can see the end of the world. It doesn't pay to think about it too much, lest you lose it. So we remain as still as we can for as long as we can, trying to take it all in. We want to remember it forever…the colors and the brightness of the light, the warmth or coldness of the day, the breeze or wind or stillness. We want to remember it all, but mostly we will remember the wonder.

SOMETHING AND NOT NOTHING

Why is the universe here? It is the basic question of existence, and philosophers have tried to answer it for generations. Why is there something and not nothing? And since there is something, is there a reason for all that we see and experience? Or, as some say, is it all the random outcome of an eternal game of chance?

In Genesis, Moses wrote a simple answer to this great existential question. The universe and all that is in it are here because God created everything that exists. Before Genesis 1:1, there was nothing except God. Then God, through the sheer power of his will, love, and grace, made out of nothing our world and everything in it and around it. God, as the teaching of the Trinity reminds us, exists in the plurality of being. That is, there is more God than can be contained in one expression or person, so the One God exists in the three Persons of the Father, Son, and Holy Spirit.

One way to understand creation is to see it as the overflow of the love that exists within the Trinity. The Father loves the Son, who loves the Father, who loves the Spirit, who loves the Son, who loves the Spirit, who loves the Father. In trying to explain the Trinity, the ancient church fathers used the Greek word *perichoresis,* or "the circle dance." They were trying to capture the image of the fast-twirling folk dances of the villages around them and use that picture as a metaphor for God. This is God, they would say: Father, Son and Holy Spirit dancing in the joy of pure love, moving so fast that you can't tell one from the other. Creation came out of the overflow of this joy. God desired an object on which to focus his love.

In a handful of verses that can be read in a matter of minutes, Moses, with some of the most beautiful poetry ever written, captures the glory, wonder, and power of the creation story. Sadly, too many people have trampled over the opening chapters of the Bible trying to find support for various theological positions or trying to impose a modern, scientific understanding of the world on Moses's words. Like a freshman English-comp class reading Robert Frost's "Stopping by Woods on a Snowy Evening" and massacring the poem as they try to squeeze out a theme for an assigned essay, many scientists, philosophers, theologians, and preachers have stomped through these chapters trying to land on the one argument that proves beyond a doubt the truth of creation.

THE "YES" OF GENESIS

Doing this is like diagramming the sentences in a love note from your spouse or sweetheart to glean leads on a good mutual fund. You'd be using the text for something that was never intended by the writer.

Moses was not trying to prove creation or even provide a detailed account of how creation happened. As the writer of Genesis, he would have seen creation as self-evident. He knew, although with limited understanding, that the world was here. In his age, philosophers weren't having coffee while debating if the cups they were drinking out of really existed. Creation was here. You could touch it, feel it, smell it. How it got here wasn't a concern. God's ways are not our ways, so Moses never bothered with the particulars of how.

Modern readers are influenced by a cultural confidence in science.

We have made amazing progress in finding cures for diseases that only a few generations ago were fatal to millions of people. NASA landed men on the moon in 1969. During the thirty-year space shuttle program, NASA sent 355 people into space and brought them safely back to earth.[1]

So modern readers get frustrated with the book of Genesis because it doesn't answer the questions that naturally come to mind. In our desire to nail down all the answers, we try to squeeze meaning from words and descriptions that were never intended to supply scientific proof. I'm sure if we could talk to Moses, he would be frustrated with us for demanding answers to questions he never intended to answer.

Few moments in literature are as powerful and expansive, glorious and awe inspiring, as the opening verses of Genesis. Few lines of poetry written anywhere are as brilliant as these. Read them again. I am using the King James Version to highlight the poetic nature of the language.

In the beginning God created the heaven and the earth. And the earth was without form, and void; and darkness was upon the face of the deep. And the Spirit of God moved upon the face of the waters. And God said, Let there be light: and there was light. And God saw the light, that it was good: and God divided the light from the darkness. And God called the light Day, and the darkness he called Night. And the evening and the morning were the first day.

And God said, Let there be a firmament in the midst of the waters, and let it divide the waters from the waters. And God made the firmament, and divided the waters which were under the firmament from the waters which were above the firmament: and it was so. And God called the firmament Heaven. And the evening and the morning were the second day.

And God said, Let the waters under the heaven be gathered together unto one place, and let the dry land appear: and it was so. And God called the dry land Earth; and the gathering together of the waters called he Seas: and God saw that it was good. And God said, Let the earth bring forth grass, the herb yielding seed, and the fruit tree yielding fruit after his kind, whose seed is in itself, upon the earth: and it was so. And the earth brought forth grass, and herb yielding seed after his kind, and the tree yielding fruit, whose seed was in itself, after his kind: and God saw that it was good. And the evening and the morning were the third day.

And God said, Let there be lights in the firmament of the heaven to divide the day from the night; and let them be for signs, and for seasons, and for days, and years: And let them be for lights in the firmament of the heaven to give light upon the earth: and it was so. And God made two great lights; the greater light to rule the day, and the lesser light to rule the night: he made the stars also. And God set them in the firmament of the heaven to give light upon the earth, And to rule over the day and over the night, and to divide the light from the darkness: and God saw that it was good. And the evening and the morning were the fourth day.

And God said, Let the waters bring forth abundantly the moving creature that hath life, and fowl that may fly above the earth in the open firmament of heaven. And God created great whales, and every living creature that moveth, which the waters brought forth abundantly, after their kind, and every winged fowl after his kind: and God saw that it was good. And God blessed them, saying, Be fruitful, and multiply, and fill the waters in the seas, and let fowl multiply in the earth. And the evening and the morning were the fifth day.

And God said, Let the earth bring forth the living creature after his kind, cattle, and creeping thing, and beast of the earth after his kind: and it was so. And God made the beast of the earth after his kind, and cattle after their kind, and every thing that creepeth upon the earth after his kind: and God saw that it was good.

And God said, Let us make man in our image, after our likeness: and let them have dominion over the fish of the sea, and over the fowl of the air, and over the cattle, and over all the earth, and over every creeping thing that creepeth upon the earth. So God created man in his own image, in the image of God created he him; male and female created he them. And God blessed them, and God said unto them, Be fruitful, and multiply, and replenish the earth, and subdue it: and have dominion over the fish of the sea, and over the fowl of the air, and over every living thing that moveth upon the earth.

And God said, Behold, I have given you every herb bearing seed, which is upon the face of all the earth, and every tree, in the which is the fruit of a tree yielding seed; to you it shall be for meat. And to every beast of the earth, and to every fowl of the air, and to every thing that creepeth upon the earth, wherein there is life, I have given every green herb for meat: and it was so. And God saw every thing that he had made, and, behold, it was very good. And the evening and the morning were the sixth day.

Thus the heavens and the earth were finished, and all the host of them. And on the seventh day God ended his work which he had made; and he rested on the seventh day from all his work which he had made. And God blessed the seventh day, and sanctified it: because that in it he had rested from all his work which God created and made.[2]

The creation text was born in the oral tradition. This story was told over and over, from one generation to the next, verbatim, for hundreds of years before it was written down. Some might see this as evidence of how unreliable the process has been in bringing our Scriptures to us. But we have evidence of oral cultures being extremely accurate in their telling and retelling of ancient stories. It was not unusual in the Middle Ages to find a rabbi who could quote the entire Old Testament from memory. Thus, Moses put together these verses of Genesis in the best possible way to be remembered by the ear, not the eye. Anyone who writes can tell you that we write differently for the eye than we do the ear. The eye and ear deal differently with words. A simple example is to read a novel, then read a screenplay for a movie based on the novel. Eyes and ears look for different things in the way a story is told.

HEARING GENESIS

Want to try something? Read the text from Genesis silently but slowly. Pay attention to the way the words are placed and how they are used in relation to one another. Then read the text out loud. Again, read slowly. Let your ears sample each sound, and notice the rhythm patterns that emphasize the meaning of the passage. Did you hear how the poet repeated the words "And God said…"? How could you miss it? It's like a hammer pounding on an anvil.

- And God said, "Let there be"…and there was!
- And God said, "It is good!"
- God spoke, and creation is here, because God spoke it into being.

God is so far beyond our comprehension that he exists only in plurality, and he speaks into being the image in his mind and the desire of his heart. He loved his work so much that he declared the seventh day a Sabbath, a day of rest, just so he would have a chance to sit back and enjoy his creation. Too many of us see the Sabbath as punishment, as if God is putting us in time-out. Nothing could be further from the truth! The Sabbath is a gift. It's a time to enjoy God, one another, and God's creation. He gave us his creation as a place where relationships happen. This is the place where love happens.

My desktop background is a picture taken from the end of the pier at my father's lake house. To me it's the most beautiful place in the world. Something about sitting in a chair and watching the river flow by calms my soul. The only thing better than sitting out there by myself is sitting there with my family or friends. Something about the slow-moving river and the mountains in the distance allows conversations to go deep and slow. This is where my dad tells his stories and where my sons feel safe enough to tell me what's going on in their lives at soul-deep levels. This is where I can hold my wife's hand and have a long conversation with her... and use just a few words. Sure, these things could happen anywhere, but they don't. They only happen when the river makes us sit down long enough to listen—to ourselves, to one another, and to the God who made it all.

GOD AS CREATOR

One of the most interesting aspects of the creation story is how God chooses to introduce himself to his world. He doesn't reveal himself as Redeemer, Savior, Healer, or Law-Giver but as Creator. If we don't know anything else about God, the opening verses of Genesis seem to say this: God is creative. He loves to make things. He ends every creative act with his own private celebration: "This is good!" The sun and the moon—good! The sea and the stars—good!

The creation scene is almost a cosmic dance of joy and laughter, with universes jumping like sparks from the fingertips of God. Worlds are spun into their orbits; stars catch fire and light the distant night; animals and plants—odd and wonderful, beautiful and confusing—find their places in God's world. Some of the animals are strange looking, almost comic. Would any of us have thought of an ostrich? Yet God points specifically to the ostrich when he responds to Job, as if he is especially proud of this awkward animal.[3]

God is the Great Artist, and as an artist, God loves to share his creations and point out great moments of beauty. So God places human beings in the center of the story, in the garden, where God will come and walk. At first God and the man talk about what Adam has learned and how he and Eve are tending the garden. God seems to want Adam to discover things, to find out what is underneath all the layers of the world around him. "Come, let me show you," we can hear God say to Adam. "Look at this! Did you find this flower or see this animal today? Tell me what you found today!"

JOY OF DISCOVERY

I think that is one of the reasons we get so excited about discovering things. Scientific breakthroughs become instant news and win international prizes. Chemists and biologists, physicists, astronomers, and paleontologists study and work in relative obscurity until they find something that changes the way we understand our world.

"Here is the way gravity works," a scientist will say. "Here is how a comet orbits through our galaxy," another will write, and from that moment on, those scientists' names become part of our everyday conversation. I recently saw a quote by British physicist Stephen Hawking in *Scientific American.* Hawking, who was addressing an audience at Arizona State University about the joys of scientific discovery, said, "I wouldn't compare it to sex, but it lasts longer."[4]

Here is what I find interesting about that quote. For Hawking, scientific discovery seems to be a primal need, something men and women were created to do. He seems to find in discovery a oneness with life, a joy that can't be found elsewhere. I believe God created the world the way he did so we would be intrigued to find out more about it. I believe God wants us to know our world—everything about it—because in the end, to discover more about the world is to know more about its Creator. We study the paintings of van Gogh and see his pain. We stare at the painting on the ceiling of the Sistine Chapel, and we get insights into Michelangelo.

We watch the stars or study the inner workings of a cell under a microscope, and we learn more about the Artist who is God.

I tend to agree with John Polkinghorne, British physicist turned priest, who writes that "God didn't produce a ready-made world. He's done something cleverer than this. He's created a world able to make itself."[5] God has infused into his work the most profound aspect of himself, revealed in the opening chapter of Genesis. The Creator created a world that creates! Likewise, human beings are given the same gift and, in truth, invitation. The Creator has created a world that creates, and he filled it with people who are now invited to join the creative adventure.

I once saw a video of Jackson Pollock working. Pollock was known for modern, colorful, even explosive works. While painting, he would hold the paint in one hand, a paintbrush in the other, and he would walk around his canvas. Quickly he would sling paint against the canvas, almost attacking the white space, and then step back as if he wanted to see what the paint was going to do. When he figured that out, he would throw or spray the next color onto the painting. In some way I guess I see creation like this—God throwing life into the emptiness of space and then watching it unfold. As it unfolds, he adds, enhances, responds, and guides so that the masterpiece on the canvas ends up just as he intended.

And from the start (and continuing even now) God invites us to join him. Adam and Eve were placed in the garden to work it and to care for it. We were placed in the world to creatively engage the world so it can achieve the full potential that God placed in it. A world fully realized, tended and nursed to reveal its full glory, would reflect the essence of the One whose desire called it into being.

CREATION OR LUCK?

There are those who say that we live in a world of cosmic randomness and that this world will eventually show up. I can't buy that. The tolerances are just too tight. If our world tipped at a slightly greater angle toward the sun, no life would be possible. With less oxygen in the atmosphere, life would be impossible. Too much protein and life would be very different from what we now know.

Some scientists say the universe is the result of dumb luck. If we were to take a bag of Scrabble letters, throw them onto the floor, and find they landed in the precise order of a Shakespearean sonnet, we would not see that as luck. We would see that as rigged. The probabilities of that happening are astronomical! I understand there may have been a process in creation. This makes sense. God works through processes all the time. He chose Abraham to begin a new nation. That was a process. Jesus called disciples to be part of a new Kingdom being born into the world. That was a process.

Creation is a process that can be studied and understood, but the process isn't random. It's guided with Divine Intent. Like Scrabble letters being used to form a sentence, creation is rigged with intelligence behind it. And more than that, it is rigged to accomplish God's purposes, and his purposes won't be frustrated. God, the Great Artist, made a world that reflects and reveals the essence of who he is. His world makes known the God who made it. You would never confuse the music of Mozart with U2, because the identity of the creators is revealed in the music they created.

And what is the fun of making something if you can't show it to someone? Joy soon evaporates if it isn't shared with another. God, then, overjoyed at the wonder and excitement of his creation, wanted someone to share it with him. So he created human beings in his image. That is, they were enough like him so that all humans can relate and in some ways share what is important with God. And yet, we are different enough from him so we can be a vital part of the relationship. God made humans and gave us dominion over his creation, and that—as simple as it sounds—is the purpose of our lives. We are on earth to fulfill the dreams God had for his masterpiece: creation. This is where we work and live. Discovering, watching, making, creating, being surprised and amazed as we find out more and more about the world. Each moment of discovery holds the potential to draw from us excited cries of wonder, prompting yet another conversation with the Artist himself.

BEAUTY AND TRUTH

While the world was created to create, God did not turn creation loose to make its own rules. Our world has an amazing reliability. Atoms behave according to certain rules, planets adhere to certain expectations, and yet our world continues to be spontaneous and surprising, consistent and intriguing all at the same time.

Mathematics reminds us we live in a logical world, a world that makes sense. While this reason and rationality is sometimes hidden from us, researcher after researcher has been amazed at how wonderfully consistent our world is in its various dimensions. There is a beauty even in the formulas that describe the workings of our world. Ian Stewart makes this point in the preface of his book *Why Beauty Is Truth: A History of Symmetry.* For mathematicians, if a formula is not beautiful, then it can't be true. If a mathematical explanation is not pleasing to the eye, the hypothesis described in the formula is probably false. There is symmetry, a beautiful resemblance between the physical world described and the formula that describes it.[6]

Stewart writes, "The symmetrical relation between mathematical ideas and the physical world, like the symmetry between our sense of beauty and the most profoundly important mathematical forms, is a deep and possibly unsolvable mystery. None of us can say why beauty is truth, and truth beauty. We can only contemplate the infinite complexity of the relationship."[7]

In writing Genesis, Moses knew why beauty is truth and truth is beauty. The reason is because God is both beauty and truth, and in the creative process God infused the world with the essence of himself. His beauty and truth remain in the universe as clues, like fingerprints from his touch. When we find them, we sit back in amazement. We are doubly encouraged to keep asking questions, to keep looking, to keep finding out, confident that one day we will come to the moment when we will find the meaning of it all. (Probably not, but we will have fun trying.) A friend once preached a sermon about how God loves to play hide-and-seek because the fun of the game is in being found. Our God, Maker of heaven and earth, has left enough clues around for us to know he loves to be found.

Moses got it right. The world is here because God wanted it to be here. We are here because God wanted us to be here, to share his work, and to know him. The world doesn't have to exist. We don't either. But when God looked into the primal nothing before creation, he decided there needed to be something instead of nothing. God said "yes" right from the beginning. That first "yes" set the stage for all God's subsequent "yeses," some of them still to come.

4

God Says "Yes" a Lot

*Even when his "yes" sounds
like "no," it is "yes"*

> He decreed statutes for Jacob and established the law in
> Israel, which he commanded our ancestors to teach their
> children, so the next generation would know them, even
> the children yet to be born, and they in turn would tell
> their children. Then they would put their trust in God
> and would not forget his deeds but would keep his
> commands.
>
> —Psalm 78:5–7

My father is a great storyteller. If you visit my family, you are going to have to listen to his stories. I've heard them all. There is a story about Aunt Hazel falling out of the car. There's a great one about how my dad tripped my mom when he first saw her at a skating rink. There is the story of Dad and his older brother, Jack, skipping school and sneaking back into the school building at night to sleep in the home economics room. (The school was heated. His house wasn't.)

When Dad tells these stories, you laugh until your sides hurt. The stories, while funny, are also poignant and etched with sadness. My father had a tough childhood, and as you listen, you understand that. But something else happens—you get to know him. In a way that facts and figures (born on this date, lived in this place) can't convey, you get to know my dad. Stories tell us about people in ways that nothing else can.

This might explain why the Bible is written as it is. Far more than a list of religious rules and divine expectations, the Bible is a collection of stories about God dealing with his people. In these stories we learn about people and events, but more than anything we learn about God.

How do so many of us miss this richness contained in the Bible? We tend to read the Bible looking for lists of dos and don'ts, or, sadly, we don't read it at all. And because we don't know the stories of God, we don't know God, which leads to our misunderstanding his intentions. Because we don't know the heart of God, we lack the context to understand his words to us. We end up thinking his laws are arbitrary rules imposed on us by an angry tyrant. But that's not true. Sure, God made laws and rules—every loving parent does—but the rules are there to protect us. The apostle John, looking for a metaphor to help the early church understand God's character, simply wrote, "God is love."[1]

The essence of God, the aspect most central to his being, is love. If God is angry, it is because something or someone he loves is threatened. More times than not, our own behavior threatens to undo us. That's why God is angered by sin. Sin threatens his children and his creation. And when we realize the threat, we get angry as well.

Don't you get angry by what you see? The hunger, poverty, abuse, rancor—all of it is driven by human sin. The very existence of our world is threatened. Doesn't that make you angry?

A God Who Feels

Honestly, I would be disappointed in God if he weren't angry. If you don't get angry, you aren't alive. One of the surprising things we discover about God is that he feels so much and so deeply. He hurts, he gets angry, he laughs...but for some reason all we focus on is his anger. God is much more complex than that. And while he does get angry, his anger does not have the final word. Grace does. Even the writers of the Old Testament knew this.

The Psalmist wrote:

For his anger lasts only a moment,
 but his favor lasts a lifetime;
weeping may stay for the night,
 but rejoicing comes in the morning.[2]

The prophet Joel made the same point:

Return to the LORD your God,
 for he is gracious and compassionate,
slow to anger and abounding in love,
 and he relents from sending calamity.[3]

Joel went as far as to say that God feels so deeply that at times he changes his mind about the punishment he was going to send. God is always looking for a way to get things back on track. He waits for opportunities to heal and forgive. Even in his punishment, there is mercy, a way out. In every "no," God finds a way to say "yes."

THE OLD TESTAMENT ON GOD'S "YES"

It's easy to misinterpret God's "yes" as being a "no." That explains much of the reason people assume God is against them, waiting in the shadows until they mess up so he can swat them. Because so many of us struggle with this, it's important to look at God's approach and to understand that his default setting is to bring redemption. No matter how much things look like a "no," God does everything possible to turn them into a "yes."

Where to begin? Why not the beginning?

None of us is surprised the original plan in the Garden of Eden didn't work out. While we might enjoy thinking about how beautiful the world would be if Adam and Eve hadn't messed up, we know it was inevitable. And we are thankful it was them and not us. Any one of us would have done much the same, giving in to the urge to do the one thing God said not to do. And think how they felt afterward. It's bad enough to mess up your own life, but to know you set in motion a rampant brokenness that would affect all people would be unbearable.

Adam and Eve blew it and were escorted from the garden. And yet, even with all of God's anger and disappointment, his response to them was measured and merciful. Yes, he sent them away, and some hard words (some even say curses) were spoken. But think about what God's words sounded like. (Remember, Genesis is written for your ears, not your eyes.)

What if God did not speak these words in anger but in tears? "Here is what I tried to protect you from. Here is what sin does. I'm sorry, but you have to leave the garden." What if this scene is more like a broken-hearted parent telling rebellious children they can't live at home any longer? What if this is the tough scene of a father standing in the driveway and giving the rebels a few bucks to get them through the next few days? But he also points out that they have become self-destructive and he just can't stand by and watch the destruction. God doesn't want to be part of our destruction. Remember, he is love.

I can feel God's hurt and disappointment. The two people he had created to have a relationship with him had rejected his love. To me, this would be a good place for God to say a loud "no," but he didn't. He found a way to say "yes."

Adam and Eve had to leave the garden, yes. But God did not leave them to their self-destruction. They had a place to live east of Eden. They had children, and the world carried on. It was not perfect. In fact, it was messy and sorrowful. Cain killed Abel. A life was lost through jealousy and violence. You would think God would have said, "That's it! I've had enough!" But he didn't. He protected Cain even as he punished him. Even here, God found a way to say "yes."

Today everything is messed up. Our relationship with God, our relationships with one another, our relationship with nature—all shot. Even with all our learning and research and discoveries about the universe, we can't fit all the pieces back together. And that is one reason we still need the stories of God, his character, his works, and his involvement with humanity. The ancient stories of creation and Adam and Eve touch something deep within us. Something in our inner beings tells us these stories are true. We long to regain what was lost. We miss what we never had, and yet we see this story lived out again and again in our lives. We know from experience that we are no better than Adam and Eve.

Noah

We see their pattern continue. In fact, after many generations things had fallen apart so badly that God regretted making the world. Humanity, for all its inherent potential, seemed to do little more than think up new ways to be evil. This is another moment when I would expect God to reach for the button marked "Total Destruction" and blow everything up. That way, he could start over. But he didn't. Instead, he said "yes" again. He found a way to overcome the self-destructive bent of the people he had created.

He began by finding a person who would be instrumental in bringing about his next "yes." He found Noah. In a time when there wasn't much good to say about the world, Noah was a good man, maybe the last of his kind. Noah took God's command seriously and built his famous boat. The entire time he was building it, he preached about the coming judgment. And no one listened. Again, you would think God might just walk away from the whole mess. But he didn't. He remembered Noah.

Noah and his family survived the Flood. His sons moved away to build their lives, and humanity had another chance. You would think after surviving the Flood, people would never forget the power of God. I guess they did remember, for a while. The Flood washed away a lot of things, but it didn't touch the hearts of human beings. If the world was going to change, it would have to begin with changed hearts. It had to come from the inside out.

So once again God gave humanity another chance.

Abraham

The next chance came through a man named Abraham. God called Abraham (then known as Abram) to leave his home and wander around until he found a new land, where he would start a new people. This was essential, because God planned to use this new nation—created by God—to bless the entire world.

Abraham and Sarah (then known as Sarai), following God's promises, took off across the wilderness to find a place they had not seen before. You would think that, being the "father of faith," Abraham would have had it all together. He didn't. As he moved into the new territory, he was afraid the kings in the area would kill him and take Sarah for themselves. So this great man of faith did what any of us would do. He lied. He told everyone Sarah was his sister. Not once but twice! Both times the kings brought Abraham into their courts to confront him with his lies. You would think he would learn, but he didn't. Still, God was working to find a way to say "yes."

The promise to Abraham was that God would make his descendants a great nation. One problem, though. Abraham and Sarah didn't have any children. How could there be a great nation of descendants when there wasn't even one? While Abraham (who was one hundred) and Sarah (who was ninety) couldn't imagine a child being born to them, a child was indeed born. Isaac, the child of the promise, would inherit God's "yes" to Abraham and, by extension, to the world. But while Abraham now had his son of promise, it didn't solve the problem of humanity's self-destructive tendencies.

Yet God kept moving forward, taking the initiative to meet needs and solve the problems that arose. He kept working, forgiving, and loving. There had to be a way. God would make sure of it.

Jacob

Esau and Jacob were Abraham's grandsons and heirs to the promise of God, but neither of them deserved it. Esau was a brute of a man. He was crude and shallow, caring nothing for the things of God. And Jacob, a lying manipulator, was no prize himself. As the story unfolds in Genesis, you get the feeling that events have finally checkmated God. Whom will he use—the hairy oaf who cares more about feeding his stomach than protecting his own birthright or the slippery schemer who can't be trusted?

God had made a promise to Abraham, and in a testimony to divine power, not humanity's faithfulness, God found a way to keep it. While Jacob was far from a perfect candidate, he was available. So God worked with what he had. In a series of events, God showed Jacob how he was working in and through Jacob's life, even when Jacob wasn't aware of it. And just to show that God wasn't afraid to get his hands dirty, God jumped Jacob on the banks of a river. They wrestled all night, with Jacob refusing to give in until he received a blessing. Jacob lived to tell about the famous wrestling match, but he limped for the rest of his life. He came away from the riverbank exhausted, lame, and bearing a new name, Israel. Once more God showed he would find a way to say "yes." When he decided how to keep his plans for humanity moving ahead, he had the power to get it done.

Moses

God's people, the Israelites, were a great nation in numbers but were enslaved by the Pharaoh of Egypt. Again it looked as if God's plan had been shut down. How can a nation of slaves become the nation to bless the entire world? But God had not run out of "yeses," and Moses was sent to emancipate God's people from their life of servitude. And who was this emancipator? He had been a Hebrew child nursed by a Hebrew mother, but he grew up as the child of Pharaoh's daughter. He was educated and trained as if he were royalty. Then he murdered an Egyptian and had to run for his life into the wilderness. After spending forty years in obscurity with a Bedouin family, Moses was sent by God to lead a nation now numbering some six hundred thousand men, plus women and children.[4] Some estimates say there were two million or more Hebrews enslaved by this time.

By his own account, Moses was the last person God should use for such a critical mission. He wasn't much of a leader, he had baggage, he wasn't a good public speaker… On and on the list went. What was most curious was that Moses didn't seem to be pointing out his many deficiencies due to false humility. Everything he said about himself was true!

Now think about the challenge he was facing. God wanted him to stand up to Pharaoh, the most powerful man on earth, and tell him to release all the slaves to Moses's care. Then, after twisting the king's arm to get him to free the slaves, Moses had to lead a vast multitude of unruly, disorganized former slaves across miles of desert to a land already occupied by powerful kingdoms.

This is not the right job description for someone who lacks confidence, can't sway a crowd with his persuasive words, and can't control his temper. In fact, the frustrations of dealing with a people who were extremely difficult cost Moses the opportunity to enter the Promised Land himself. But God used Moses anyway. By the time the Hebrews were safely out of Egypt, Pharaoh had been humiliated repeatedly, the Egyptian people had given the slaves great riches to carry with them, and much of the Egyptian army had drowned in the Red Sea. When God says "yes," he means it.

Paul reminds us that God chooses people who are overlooked by the world to accomplish his purposes.[5] Moses is exhibit A. Here's the point that is made again and again: even when there is good reason for God to say "no," he chooses "yes." Then he finds a way—working with highly flawed people—to accomplish his plans.

The prophets

Each of the prophets in his own way is a portrait of God's "yes." We tend to see the prophets as overly intense men with sweaty red faces and bulging veins screaming hellfire and brimstone to the wicked people of Israel. We would do much better, though, to understand them as men who wept and preached more out of broken hearts than angry ones. Each of the prophets used different ways to emphasize the same message: if you turn back to God, he will turn to you, and in turning you will find healing and hope not only for you and your family but also for the whole nation. There is always a way out. There is always a way to get your life turned around.

THE NEW TESTAMENT ON GOD'S "YES"

The ministry of Jesus literally fleshed out the "Divine Yes" of God. Whether he was working with his disciples or responding to the crowds, Jesus's message was the same: God is still working to fulfill the dreams he had for creation when he called everything into being. His purposes are not going to be frustrated by anything or anyone.

The people who first responded to Jesus's call may not have been the obvious choices, but the fact that they responded made them just the kind of people Jesus could use. They were a big part of God's "yes."

Peter

Simon Peter is a prime example of an unlikely follower of Jesus. I think the reason Peter is so prominent in Christian tradition is because all of us identify with him. He loved Jesus passionately, and he failed famously. He challenged Jesus to allow him to walk on water to his Master. When

Jesus agreed, Peter took a few steps and then panicked. He would have drowned if Jesus had not pulled him up. It's just about impossible to read that story and not see ourselves sinking into the Sea of Galilee alongside Peter.

How many promises have we made to Jesus only to almost drown because of our unbelief? Peter later promised Jesus he would not desert him, no matter what. Then Jesus was arrested, and Peter tagged along at a distance. The disciple stopped to warm himself at a fire in the courtyard of the high priest's residence, and when Peter was challenged as being one of Jesus's disciples, he denied he even knew who Jesus was. Not once, but three times.

We read that tragic story, and our hearts ache with recognition. Been there. Done that. But we keep reading, because Peter is part of God's "yes." Peter's story doesn't end with this rank betrayal.

If there was going to be a time when Jesus would give up on the people he came to save, you would think this would be it. Simon Peter had been with him from the beginning. Peter should have known Jesus, should have understood who he really was. But Peter could not summon the courage to stand with his Master. He failed Jesus and ran away in shame. Luke tells us there was eye contact between Jesus and Peter in the courtyard after the disciple's betrayal. Then Peter left, and later the soldiers took Jesus away to be tortured and crucified.[6] The last real contact Peter had with Jesus, prior to Jesus's resurrection, was that look.

So on Easter Sunday morning when the women returned from the tomb and announced, "Jesus is alive," it must have been great news to everybody but Peter. He had denied Jesus, and now the women were saying the angel told them that Jesus was waiting for Peter specifically. What would Jesus say about Peter's denial?

Several of the disciples had been fishermen prior to being called by Jesus. After his crucifixion they returned to the sea to practice their trade. Peter and John were in a boat and noticed a man onshore. They realized it was Jesus. I imagine Peter felt his heart sink when he saw Jesus on the same shore where Peter had first seen him three years before. Peter, the bragging fisherman, the cocky disciple, the big talker, was now a man broken on the anvil of reality.

Peter stood before Jesus, whom he loved more than anything but had betrayed completely. Perhaps they looked at each other much the same way they had in the courtyard before the crucifixion. And after their breakfast that morning, Jesus asked Peter again and again, "Simon, do you love me?" Each time in his feeble way Peter tried to respond. Jesus was taking Peter back to the first moment he had made a decision to become a disciple of Christ (when he was still Simon, the brother of Andrew). For each time the rooster had crowed, and for each time Peter had denied his Lord, Jesus gave him a chance to affirm his love once more.[7]

I don't know many people who have gone to the great lengths to restore a relationship that Jesus did to find Peter and restore him to the ministry. Jesus did not just say "yes" to Peter; he said it three times—each time contradicting a "no" that Peter himself had spoken.

Paul

I doubt any of us would have chosen Saul, the young zealot, to be the leading spokesman for our message to the rest of the world. Yet God chose Saul, the persecutor of Jesus's followers, to become Paul the apostle. In a dramatic appearance as Saul was on the road to Damascus, Jesus changed Saul's name and his destiny. As Saul, a leading Pharisee, he devoted his energies to attacking churches. After meeting Jesus, he became the man who started churches throughout the Roman Empire.

Saul lived by the word "no." He saw a new faith emerging as people followed the life and teachings of Jesus, said to be the Jewish Messiah. Saul's entire being was devoted to killing this heresy. But Jesus saw Saul and what he had to offer, and Jesus said "yes."

Years later Paul set forth on one of the most surprising expressions of "yes" ever written. Onesimus, a runaway slave, met Paul. Under Paul's teaching, Onesimus became a Christian, and questions came up regarding his escape from his master. Paul wrote a letter that was carried by Onesimus back to his owner, Philemon.

Philemon knew Paul, and Paul obviously considered Philemon a friend. Paul felt comfortable talking openly with his friend about the runaway Onesimus, now a brother in Christ. Paul wrote, "I am sending Onesimus back to you although I could keep him here with me to help me in my ministry. Yet, while I am sending him back, I am sending him back as a brother, not a slave."[8] Paul didn't explicitly tell Philemon to release his slave, but he used enough leading language in the letter to make us understand that Paul was expecting Philemon to do just that. After all, how could anyone hold a brother as a slave?

This is an odd letter in many ways. Some scholars have questioned why the short letter of Philemon is even in the Bible. It doesn't deal with any critical theological issues. It's highly personal. It was not written to a church but to an individual. But for me, it's a short version of the gospel. A runaway finds salvation, a slave finds freedom—that is the message of Christ that Paul preached throughout the Roman Empire. Onesimus was living proof.

There's another reason I think the letter to Philemon is found in the New Testament. In the early church a bishop collected all of Paul's letters for the church to keep. That bishop's name? Onesimus. We have no way of knowing if the bishop was the slave in Paul's letter, but it makes a great story. Picture the bishop rolling together the scrolls containing Paul's letters to Christians in Corinth and Galatia and other cities. Then he folds his own letter in there to make sure the world will know the story of a slave who ran away only to find his "yes" in Christ.

The "yes" of Revelation

The book of Revelation would seem, at least at first reading, to fall into the category of a "no" book. It paints a terrifying picture of the ultimate judgment of the world in the great Battle of Armageddon. What could that be but God's final, violent rejection of all he had created? Yet this vision of the Apocalypse is John's message to believers who were struggling under the oppression and persecution of the Roman Empire. John wanted them to remain faithful despite their hardships. Why? Because the God who spoke the first word will be the same God who speaks the last word. That last word spoken will be the same word spoken at the beginning: "Yes!"

The Bible begins and ends with God's most affirming word. Despite all the human failures, despite the open rebellion of humanity against its Creator, God patiently and persistently weaves his will into the lives of men and women who are open to his presence. Nothing can distract God from fulfilling his will. And his will is guided by "yes." The Bible ends with God being as excited for the completion of his creation as he was at its beginning.

MORE COULD BE SAID

When you read the biblical story, you'll see time after time that God easily could have said "no," and situations could have caused him to draw the line and declare, "That's enough! I've had it!" Yet he never did. God kept finding a way to say "yes." He continues his "yes" today, tomorrow, and forever. God keeps working in whoever will give him a chance. Rahab was a prostitute in Jericho, but she allied herself with God's spies, and more than three millenniums later we still celebrate her as a heroine of the faith. She made a living by selling her body. Who on earth would have chosen her? No one on earth would, but God did.

Ruth, Naomi, Esther, Mary, and Martha—these women had very little standing in their ancient societies, but God knew their value and called them into service. Their hearts were open to him, and he moved in their lives. They are known today as crucial components in God's working out his Divine Yes.

The church in Philippi was started because a woman named Lydia responded to Paul's preaching and answered God's "yes" with a "yes" of her own. There are so many of these stories and enough detail in them for us to see a pattern. God has decided to overcome every "no" of humanity with his powerful and persistent "yes." We serve a God who takes initiative, who sees problems and creates solutions. God sent his Son, Jesus Christ, to live out the Divine Yes in front of us.

I have left out a lot in this fast-paced overview of God's working in the world. But even a quick glance at history shows God's heart is aimed at drawing us near to him, calling us to himself, providing solution after solution when we reject his overtures. God never stops saying "yes" to the ones he loves. God is still working out his Divine Yes, and, as before, he is looking for people who will join him in this work. You don't have to be perfect to be chosen by God. You just have to answer "yes" when you hear his call.

The "Yes"
of the Cross

*God's greatest "yes" was
also the most costly*

For the joy set before him [Jesus] endured the cross,
scorning its shame, and sat down at the right hand of
the throne of God.

—HEBREWS 12:2

Jamie did not grow up in the church. He comes from a nonreligious family on the Eastern seaboard. His parents never said they didn't believe in God, but then again, they never said they did believe. When the matter of God would come up around Christmas and Easter, a few opinions would be offered, and then someone would change the subject, and it wouldn't be mentioned again.

Jamie moved to Nashville to start his first job out of college, and friends invited him to attend a worship service designed for young professionals. After coming to the services for a few weeks, he sent me an e-mail. He wondered if I would mind having a cup of coffee with him so we could talk about some questions he had. "I would be glad to," I told him, and we agreed on a time and place.

A FEW QUESTIONS

After a few minutes of conversation about how a born New Yorker was adapting to life in Music City, Jamie put down his coffee and leaned back in his chair. "Do you mind if I ask you a few questions?"

"Not at all," I said.

"I have been coming to Kairos [a service for young adults at our church], and I really like the services. You've said some things that got me thinking, but I can't figure some things out."

"Like what?" I asked.

"Like…" He looked away from me as he thought about it. Then he rocked forward in his chair and landed hard on his elbows. "Like the whole thing. I don't get any of it."

I smiled and said, "Don't feel too bad. I've been studying this stuff all my life, and there are parts I still don't get. That's why we call it a mystery. You can't figure it out, not all of it anyway. Our brains just aren't big enough."

"I get that Jesus lived. I don't have any problem with that. I get that he was really smart and we would do better if we listened to him."

I said, "You seem to have it down better than most of my church members."

He went on, "But there is a lot I just can't get to make sense."

"Such as?"

"Okay, so Jesus was God's Son, right?"

"Right."

"So how does God have a Son? Is that what Mary was for?"

"You have just hit on a couple of the most difficult themes in Christian theology, the Trinity and the Incarnation."

"Great. Seems like I just jumped into the deep end of the pool," Jamie said, rubbing his head with both hands.

"Well, we have to start somewhere. Where do you want to start?"

"Just start," he said. "I'm so confused I wouldn't know the beginning from the end."

I reached for a napkin and took out a pen. "Sometimes it helps me if I think about this as a problem that God was trying to solve. Humanity had drifted from God, and God wanted to bring them back, and the only way he could do that was to send Jesus into the world."

I drew a vertical line down the center of the napkin.

"What do we know about God? We know God is just and holy. He has firm rules about what is right and wrong."

"Like the Ten Commandments," Jamie said.

"Yeah, like the Ten Commandments. God gave us ten rules for living, with the understanding that we can never break those ten laws."

"But we blew them all up."

"That's right. Now, God is a loving God, but he is also just. He cannot ignore sin, because sin hurts his children. God tries to protect us by giving us laws—rules to live by—like 'Don't play in the street.' So what happens when we break the rules?"

"We get in trouble?"

"Big trouble. The kind of trouble we can't get out of. In fact, the apostle Paul wrote in the book of Romans, "The wages of sin is death."[1] And in small ways, we know this is true. If you lie, what happens?"

"Nobody believes you anymore," he said.

"That's right. Integrity dies. If you lie, character dies. Something dies every time someone sins. Sometimes the deaths are big and you can't miss them, like when a rock star loses everything because of a drug habit. Other times the deaths are little, like telling white lies to your wife to the extent she doesn't listen to you anymore. But they are deaths just the same."

"Do the crime. Do the time."

"You've got it, and here's the problem. We can't fix what we messed up. We can't ever make it right again."

"We can't fix what we messed up?"

"No matter how hard we try. Now you see God's first problem. He loves us, but in our messing up, starting with Adam and Eve, people have been hurt. Crimes have been committed. Yes, God is loving, but everyone knows we are guilty. If God doesn't address this, well, right and wrong have no meaning." I pointed at the vertical line I had drawn. On the left side of the line I wrote the word *God*. On the right side I wrote *Us*. "So what does a just and holy God say to a sinful people?"

"Firing squad?"

I chuckled at his honesty. "That's one of God's options. He could simply enforce the death penalty. And what happens if God enforces the death penalty?"

"It's all over."

"God has had plenty of chances to say 'no,' but he keeps finding a way to say 'yes.' If it were just a question of right and wrong, then it would be a simple, open-and-shut case. But God is more than just a Divine Judge of Right and Wrong. He is also our Creator. Jesus said God is our Father. So how would a perfect Father handle this situation?"

Jamie smiled. "I don't know, but I have a feeling the answer is Jesus."

"Right. The answer is Jesus. But you have to understand why Jesus is the right answer."

I put my pen near the spot on the napkin where I had written *God* and drew a horizontal line across to *Us*. The result was a cross with *God* at one end of the cross's horizontal arm and *Us* at other end. "God is merciful, but how does he show mercy without compromising his justice? How does he give us a way out without discounting the harm caused by our sin? The answer is that God decided to satisfy the demands of justice himself. In his Son, Jesus Christ, God paid the price we can't pay for ourselves."

"So Jesus died for us."

"Yes, and, more than that, he lived for us, and even now he lives for us in his resurrection. God became human in Jesus. God affirmed the tremendous worth of humanity by entering into the human experience; Jesus became one of us and lived in our world. He ate our food, walked our roads, and felt our pain. He knew what it was to be a person who was limited in the physical realm. He got tired and hungry, experienced confusion and betrayal—just as we do. In every way he experienced the reality of life as a human being in our world."

"But Jesus didn't mess up."

"Exactly. Even when he was tempted, ridiculed, and tortured, Jesus responded just as God the Father wanted him to. And that perfect life was the payment offered to answer the demands of justice. Jesus lived a perfect life, so he had done nothing that deserved execution, but he was executed anyway. He died everybody else's death. Justice has been satisfied."

I pointed to the intersection of the two lines on the napkin. "We are invited to accept Jesus's death on our behalf. We are urged to substitute his execution for ours so we will not be sentenced to death. This is God's mercy offered to us. By taking Jesus's death as our own, we are given a way out. Jesus died once for everybody who deserved to die. He died at the place where the justice of God and the mercy of God meet, at the heart of the cross."

MERCY AND JUSTICE

How does God temper his justice with mercy? The answer is Jesus, the God-Man. Fully God, Jesus entered into our lives; fully human, he offers a way out through his invitation to follow him.

God said "no" to sin because it violates his holiness, but wanting us not to break his laws is not his number-one reason for opposing sin. He hates sin because it destroys the people he loves. Jesus took into himself the "no" of our sin and died in God's mercy so we might find our "yes" in him. As he prayed in the Garden of Gethsemane, as blood oozed out in his sweat, Jesus asked for the cup of suffering to be taken from him. This cup was the "no" we so rightfully deserved. But the cup was not taken from Jesus. He took our "no" and offered back his life of "yes," securing our salvation. "Greater love has no one than this: to lay down one's life for one's friends."[2]

We forget how devastating sin can be. Sometimes when I talk to friends, they tell me about a bad decision or a series of bad decisions they made years ago that had a life-altering outcome. Relationships were broken and couldn't be put back together. Opportunities were squandered; offers of help were rejected; people who loved them were betrayed. They look at me as if I have some kind of magic power to take them back to the moment when the mistake was made so they can do things differently this time. But some things, once done, can't be undone. There are mistakes that regret, confession, and requests for forgiveness can't fix.

Some people wrongly conclude their lives are over, and they give in to a self-destructive lifestyle. Others change something. They get a different job, move to another city, change churches, doing anything they can think of in an attempt to get a second chance. The problem is this: wherever they go, they take themselves. What good is a new city or a different job if it's still the same old you?

But others ask Christ for forgiveness, understanding that his death on the cross is the only sacrifice needed for their failures. They let the filling presence of Jesus wipe away the crippling guilt and self-hatred. They understand that when Christ died for them, he took upon himself not just their sin but also the pain. They give their lives to the Savior who gave his life for them. Their old lives, the people they used to be, will slowly die as they allow Christ to become more of who they are. "He must become greater," John the Baptist said as he pointed to Jesus. "I must become less."[3]

THE BEGINNING

All of us are broken. And accepting God's mercy in Christ does not magically repair the shattered pieces of life. But from the start, healing work occurs on the inside. In time, seeds planted in secret by God's Spirit will blossom into the harvest of a radically changed life. Right now, however, at least on the surface, nothing will seem to have changed. Even with Christ in us and with us, the hard circumstances of life are still there, staring us in the eyes. That's because Jesus isn't changing the situation but the person. *You* will have changed, and the reality of faith in Christ gives you new resources and strength to work on your circumstances. Putting a new person in old circumstances changes, by definition, those circumstances.

If some things need to be made right, a person with Christ's Spirit living inside will do all she can to make amends. Christianity is not an escape from the past but redemption of the past. What we see as past failures and mistakes, God will redeem for his purposes.

Let me put it another way. God will take all the "nos" in your life and find a way to make them all "yeses." This happens again and again. Someone tells me about a past decision or action that has caused great pain and shame. In telling the story, he makes me promise not to mention it to anyone. "If anyone else knew this," he says, "I would die."

So I don't tell anyone. Meanwhile, the person is working through his issues, and people can't help but notice how his life is changing. Naturally, they ask what is happening. And he starts to talk about how he came to know Christ and what that means for him now, living a new life.

I've heard friends share their testimonies later on, and what is the first line they speak? It's nearly always the very thing they were sure would kill them if anyone ever knew. Such is the goodness of our God. He can take the worst day of your life and make it the first line of your testimony of redemption.

THE COURAGE OF "YES"

How does the most shameful "no" of your life become the "yes" you are eager to talk about? It happens because Jesus makes you deal with stuff.

A long time ago I noticed a pattern. Whenever I asked Jesus to help me with a problem, he would take me right back to the problem itself. Talk about frustrating. I wanted Jesus to pick me up and toss me over to the other side so I wouldn't have to even think about the problem anymore. I wanted to look back and say, "Whew, that was close," then walk away from it.

But that's not what Jesus does. He puts me right back in front of my problem. If I am praying about a relationship with someone I can't get along with, I will run into that person every day for two weeks. If I'm struggling with a temptation, everything I read or see will relate to that particular issue.

Whenever we have a problem that needs to be addressed, Jesus will get our attention. Then he will force us to deal with the issue as he makes his power available to help us. We will have to forgive what needs to be forgiven, accept responsibility for the part of the problem that is ours, and then release the rest. Why? Because once Jesus allows you to deal with your problems, you don't have to be afraid of them anymore.

When you read the stories in Scripture, you see that God never takes his children down a safe, level road that skirts the problem. He leads them right through the problem. The Hebrew children walked through the Red Sea. Shadrach, Meshach, and Abednego walked through the fiery furnace. Jesus went through death and defeated death on death's own terms. And since he completed the work of redemption, we no longer have to be afraid of anything. Our worst enemy was faced and conquered by Christ. We can live in the freedom of his forgiveness and in his healing from now on. Paul was right when he reminded Timothy, "For the Spirit God gave us does not make us timid, but gives us power, love and self-discipline."[4]

I know people are suspicious anytime someone claims to have "found Jesus" and now to be completely forgiven. To those outside the faith, it sounds arrogant for one group to talk as if they are on special, intimate terms with God. We don't mean it to sound arrogant, because we certainly did nothing to deserve such grace. But it is true that every believer is on intimate terms with God, at God's invitation.

Of course, there are reasons for outsiders thinking a claim to know Jesus sounds hollow. Wrongdoers, after they are caught, often suddenly claim to have "found Jesus." For many criminals, finding the Lord seems like a good strategic move, at least by the time they appear in court.

And Christians have to take some of the blame for the glib way people talk about forgiveness. God's grace has been cheapened by those who claim forgiveness without showing any radical changes in their new life in Christ. If a person's life is not changed in significant, noticeable ways, then the forgiveness of Christ is not at work.

You may experience an emotional release in confessing your sins or crimes, but confession is not repentance. Confession is part of repentance, but repentance requires more. True repentance demands a change in the way a person thinks and what she now desires, which is lived out in the choices she makes.

If you understand what Christ did for you on the cross, repentance is your only valid response. When you understand the wounds in his hands and side are there because of the punishment required to pay your debt, what else can you do with that knowledge? There is only one way to respond: by giving him your life. Because we were dead men and women walking and are now offered life because of his death, we do the only thing we can do. We give our lives back to him. It's not an even exchange by any means, but it's all we can do. Our lives are no longer our own. We have been "bought at a price."[5]

ONLY ONE RESPONSE

In one of my favorite episodes of *The Andy Griffith Show*, Andy saves Gomer's life. When the gas station attendant realizes what Andy has done, he pledges his life to Andy. The rest of the episode shows Gomer getting in Andy's way, trying hard to serve the man who saved his life. "I owe you my life, Andy Taylor," Gomer keeps saying. Things get so frustrating for Andy he finally comes up with a plan for Gomer to save his life so they can be even and Gomer will finally leave him alone.

But how can you or I ever make things even with Jesus so that no more debt is owed? We can't. And if we can't pay it back, the only thing I know to do is to die trying. Now, don't get me wrong. I am not motivated to serve Christ out of guilt or obligation. I just can't find any other way to respond appropriately to his love. He is my Lord. He has bought me. He calls the shots.

My friends in real estate tell me that any piece of property is worth only what someone is willing to pay for it. I will never get over the price that God the Father was willing to pay for me and you. Our redemption cost God the price of his Son's life. That's the reason I do what I do. I guess that's why I am writing this book. I want you to know that the "yes" of Christ spoken on the cross covers whatever "no" you may have heard before.

THE "YES" OF BEING FOUND

I always laugh a little when someone tells me they found Jesus. I remind them Jesus wasn't lost; they were. Jesus found them. The Good Shepherd is still searching for and finding his lost sheep. The good news of the gospel is not that we can get to God. The good news is that God in Christ Jesus has come to us.

In the parable of the good Samaritan, Jesus tells a story about a traveler who is jumped by thieves and left for dead. A rabbi walks by and doesn't stop. A Pharisee, widely known in that culture as part of the religious leadership, walks by as well. Only one person stops, and it's a Samaritan, a social and ethnic outcast. This man was despised by faithful Jews due only to his ethnicity, but he stops and helps the victim. When preachers in the early church told this story, every person who heard it was the one who had been jumped, beaten up, robbed, and left for dead.

Everyone could identify with that. Even today, life tends to beat us up, to rob us of what matters, and to leave us in a ditch to die.

The early preachers would explain that no one will stop for us. Then, just as we are about to give up hope, a stranger stops. This Stranger is not someone we have seen before, but he is someone we know. God in his mercy would not let our pain become the last word in our lives, no matter how much we deserve it. The Stranger who stops is familiar with sorrow. He was despised and rejected. He is the One who bears the stripes that heal us.[6] Jesus stopped and paid for our lives when we'd been left for dead and had no other hope but him. We now owe him our lives.

This is Christ's "yes" to us. When the sentence was death, a sentence we deserved, he took our death as his own. He took our "no" upon himself so we would never suffer from it again. And in doing so, he has left us his "yes." We have received the "yes" of the Father through Christ the Son. Now we live our lives in order to give our "yes" back to him in adoration, praise, and service.

The "Yes"
of the Resurrection

*If Jesus had not risen from the dead,
we would be left without hope*

And last of all he appeared to me also, as to one abnormally
born.

—PAUL (1 CORINTHIANS 15:8)

I have a pet peeve with most theology books. They start at the wrong
places. The opening chapters begin with how we know things and,
thus, how we can be sure we know what we say we know about God.
They start with ontology, epistemology, or the nature of the Scriptures.

Other theologians begin with lengthy chapters on the Bible and why
we can trust what it tells us. And then there are the ones that start with
God himself. They open with an imposing chapter that takes God's
name as the chapter title. It's called "God." Well, after you explain God
in the first chapter, what is left to say?

Any good book on theology will need to address these topics and
many more. But as we approach questions of God and his dealings with
humanity, I don't think these are the best places to start. When a person
is searching and wondering if God might have the answer, he doesn't

start with an in-depth examination of whether we can trust the Bible. And tackling the topic of God in a systematic way is not the open door most of us are looking for. And then there is the confusion caused by Jesus. If any of us were going to come up with a figure to save the world, we would not begin with a helpless infant born to an unmarried teenager camping out in a barn. That's a problem, and it's one of the problems Jesus had with his contemporaries. No one thought he looked like someone God would send to earth as the promised Messiah.

You could say that the search for God's "yes" requires us to do things backward. Here's what I mean.

THE NEW REALITY

Christianity begins with the unexpected and then keeps surprising us. Rather than delving into the complexities of Scripture or pondering the imponderables of God, Christianity has as its starting point a breach of our everyday lives. Christ appears to us, unexpectedly, and the revelation of the Risen Christ blows up our world. An explosion is an apt metaphor. When Shane Claiborne described his conversion, he wrote, "Jesus wrecked my life."[1] This is the same experience reported by Saul the persecutor. He used a little different language, but that's what happened to him en route to Damascus. It's what happens to everyone who is met by Christ.

One day Jesus appears to you. Jesus is alive, and you have to make a choice. Is Jesus the real deal or not? If Jesus is the real deal, then the only choice is to follow him by giving him your life. And when you do that, everything changes.

Starting now, the things you thought were up are really down. What was down is now up. What was treasure is now trash, and trash has become treasure. What you wanted from life you no longer want. What you needed you no longer need. It's all backward and upside down.

What happened? You've been converted, transformed, changed, made new, resurrected from your own death to a new life in Christ. The old person you used to be is gone, and a new person is being created in you. You will spend the rest of your life trying to understand what happened in the moment Christ appeared to you. It will continue to amaze you and cause you to rejoice.

Paul spent three years in the Arabian Desert and Damascus trying to fully grasp the meaning of the blinding light and the Voice that came out of the light. Martin Luther and John Wesley spent the rest of their lives, through sermons and books, exploring the ramifications of Christ's resurrection. Why do you think C. S. Lewis, a professor of the classics, started writing theology? He was trying to understand God and grace and faith and redemption and much more. His desire to understand continues to help the rest of us understand.

Faith Opens the Door

Some of Jesus's modern-day critics have wondered why he didn't do more after his resurrection to prove the skeptics wrong. If he really was raised from the dead, and if that was the unassailable proof that he was sent from God, why didn't Jesus pay a visit to Pontius Pilate? Why didn't he walk into the Roman official's chamber and show that he was, in fact, the King of the Jews? And while he had the chance, why didn't Jesus appear before the Sanhedrin and prove to the religious leaders who had condemned him that he was indeed the Messiah, the Son of God? Wouldn't the ordeal of hearing from a man who had come back from the dead have been a better way to launch the new Christian faith?

Why didn't Jesus make a big noise about the resurrection? Why did he just walk away from Jerusalem and go back to the relative obscurity of the provinces to meet quietly with his disciples?

No one knows, but here are my guesses. Remember, Jesus never stayed around very long with people who didn't believe. Before his death he went to the people of Nazareth. They discounted him, and Jesus left. He never forced himself or his ministry on anyone. And after the resurrection he had no reason to change that. Faith would always open the door for Christ to come and stay with you. Unbelief would always close it.

In terms of combined time, the religious leaders in Jerusalem had been with Jesus more than just about anyone. But because of their own agenda, they never gave Jesus a chance. They made up their minds quickly that Jesus couldn't be the Messiah. And once their minds were made up, they set about looking for evidence to prove their case. They hadn't believed prior to the crucifixion, when Jesus was standing in front of them. They wouldn't have believed if Jesus had stood in front of them a second time, after his death and resurrection.

Pilate would have been the same way. His motivation had been clear from the beginning: avoid confrontation and stay in office. Jesus threatened that agenda. Regardless of how sympathetic Pilate may have been to the unjust nature of the charges brought against Jesus, he didn't believe Jesus was sent from God. His mind was made up, and he would have adjusted the facts accordingly, even if Jesus had appeared to him after his death.

Both Pilate and the religious leaders understood what it would have meant to believe that Jesus was the Christ. For the Jewish leaders, it would have shown that their Messiah had arrived, and they would have lost their positions as arbiters of right and wrong. For Pilate, it would have meant he was accepting the authority of a King other than Caesar. It would have changed everything, just as it did for Jesus's other followers.

So rather than force the issue, Jesus did what he always does. He went to the places and to the people who needed him. He had said, "It is not the healthy who need a doctor, but the sick. I have not come to call the righteous, but sinners."[2] So Jesus went to the places and the people who understood their need for him.

On the morning of the resurrection, Jesus found Mary Magdalene in the garden. He later waited for Peter on the shore of the lake. He extended his hands so Thomas could examine the wounds left by the spikes. He walked to Emmaus with Cleopas and his friend. Jesus was then, and is now, looking for people who, by faith, will give him just the slightest chance to make himself known.

And when Jesus is given a chance, everything starts to change. Bethlehem was a very small village, and a stable was certainly no place for a King to be born. Jesus didn't seem to mind. It was a good place to start. More than five thousand people followed Jesus into the countryside, and they were hungry. "Who will feed all these people?" Jesus asked. A little boy had a lunch—just a few loaves of bread and a couple of fish. It wasn't much, but it was a start.

That is all Jesus looks for—a small place to start with a person who is willing. He sought out fishermen who were willing to follow. (This is not a strategy found in most leadership books, but it was the start of a worldwide movement.) Jesus still comes to those who are willing to listen to him, willing to trust him. He can do a lot when someone will give him even a small place to start. The gospel isn't about us; it's about Jesus. The story isn't about what we can do but about what Christ can do in us and through us.

Jesus as the Divine Yes

In 2 Corinthians, Paul wrote, "For no matter how many promises God has made, they are 'Yes' in Christ. And so through him the 'Amen' is spoken by us to the glory of God."[3]

In the resurrection Christ brought into reality all the promises God had given to his people. The church confirms the work of Christ and joins him in his redemptive work on earth. And what is that work? Finding the lost, healing the sick, caring for the broken. In Mark 10 we read the story of a blind man named Bartimaeus. Jesus was leaving Jericho, and while he was walking with his disciples and other followers, Bartimaeus began to cry out. Some of those walking with Jesus told the beggar to be quiet, to stop bothering Jesus. Bartimaeus didn't care. He wanted Jesus to notice him, so he cried out louder and louder. When Jesus heard him, he told his disciples to bring the man to him, which they did.

What has always haunted me about this passage was the stinging realization that the church I am part of has, too many times, been the group that told the messed up and the desperate to be quiet. The church should be—I should be—the one who goes to the lost and confused, the messed up and despondent, telling them, "Good news! Jesus is calling for you." The same God who called Jesus back to life, who gave Bartimaeus his sight, is now calling for you. God is not finished. There is still hope. The resurrection was just the beginning.

Jesus Is the Way

The resurrection means Jesus doesn't leave us to figure out life on our own. He is here to help us find another way to live. Because of the resurrection, we have new life.

When Jesus walked on earth, people did not follow him because he condemned them but because he offered them a way out. Jesus didn't condemn the woman caught in adultery, but he did tell her to stop sinning.[4] Christ finds us where we are, but as the old preachers say, "Thank God he doesn't leave us there." Like Peter and John, Andrew and James, and all of those before us, we are called to leave our present lives and commit to a new life in a new future. We leave our old selves, and we are transformed by the Truth, the Ultimate Reality we find in Christ. The transformation Christ brings involves the total person—thoughts, desires, choices. Everything is brought under the lordship, or rule, of Christ.

Once, after Jesus was teaching some difficult truths about the cost of being a disciple, most of the crowd walked away. They were either unwilling or unable to pay the price to follow. Jesus was left not with a crowd but with twelve men. " 'You do not want to leave too, do you?' Jesus asked the Twelve. Simon Peter answered him, 'Lord, to whom shall we go? You have the words of eternal life.'"[5]

Peter nailed it. Where else could we go to get what Christ alone has to give? Who else has come from God and thus knows the way back to God? Who else has conquered death? Jesus knows something about life that no one else knows. Dallas Willard wrote:

> He [Christ] is not just nice, he is brilliant. He is the smartest
> man who ever lived. He is now supervising the entire course
> of world history (Rev. 1:5) while simultaneously preparing
> the rest of the universe for our future role in it (John 14:2).
> He always has the best information on everything and cer-
> tainly also on those things that matter most in human life.
> Let us now hear his teachings on who has the good life, on
> who is among the truly blessed.[6]

Jesus understands life at its deepest levels better than anyone else. Because his truth is based on the unchanging, transcendent truth of God, Jesus can teach us what no one else can. "In the beginning was the Word [Jesus Christ], and the Word was with God, and the Word was God."[7] Who else has that kind of inside information about ultimate reality?

JESUS AS THE ULTIMATE YES

Jesus is more than a good teacher. Because he has been raised from the dead, he is the ultimate authority on truth in every aspect of life. If we want a clear picture of reality and a clear and accurate understanding of life, we have to look at it through the lens of Jesus. The Risen Christ makes us rethink everything. If God chose to take on human flesh and live among us, and then die for us, and then defeat death by being raised from the dead, we have to acknowledge that it would be foolish to try to live without his wisdom and power at work in us. Seen in this light, Jesus's teachings take on another dimension.

Take the Beatitudes. If Jesus is just a teacher, the Beatitudes are inspirational moral goals to which we should aspire. But if Jesus is alive, the Beatitudes become the moral expectations of the coming Kingdom to which we must conform. What about his miracles? If Christ is risen, the miracles become glimpses into the future Kingdom, sneak peeks at the coming reality of eternity.

We understand God most fully through what Jesus said about the Father and how Jesus revealed the Father's heart through his obedience to his Father's will. Remember Jesus's response to his disciple Philip?

> "If you really know me, you will know my Father as well. From now on, you do know him and have seen him."
>
> Philip said, "Lord, show us the Father and that will be enough for us."
>
> Jesus answered: "Don't you know me, Philip, even after I have been among you such a long time? Anyone who has seen me has seen the Father. How can you say, 'Show us the Father'?"[8]

To have seen Jesus is to have seen the Father himself. To know Jesus is to know the Father as well as the place of Scripture in our lives and the reason the church exists. In knowing Jesus, and the Father through Jesus, we understand the history of Israel, the Creation and Fall, the problem of sin, and the glory of salvation, hope, and love. All of life—from struggles and failures to mercy, grace, and celebration—is understood *only* through the person of Jesus Christ.

John opens his gospel with the famous line "In the beginning was the Word."[9] One definition of *logos,* or "word," is "meaning." Another way to read the opening verse of John is this: "In the beginning was the Meaning." Jesus is the meaning. He is the defining reality of everything.

The Beginning of "Yes"

That's why I'm convinced that every theology book should begin with the resurrection, which is God's ultimate "yes" to humanity. In Christ, death has been defeated and meaning has been restored to our living. Death is the final negation of life. Christ is the living proof of life beyond death, of hope and meaning beyond death. That changes everything.

In his book *The Present Future,* Reggie McNeal points out that it's a mistake to think the present has come from the past.[10] The reality is much more radical than that. The coming Kingdom of God is so close, the future reign of Christ is pushing in on our present so intensely, we have to shift our allegiance to the only reigning King. Christ-followers are called, in the present, to live the future ethic of the coming Kingdom. Love is the currency of the coming Kingdom of heaven. Love is strong enough to mold the present confusion into the glory of God's Kingdom, and it is the power that drives our living now.

We serve the God who made all creation from nothing. As we live on earth in light of his Kingdom, we serve a God who is making all things new,[11] starting with the brokenness in our lives, homes, communities, and nations. His love bears all things, and his love never fails.[12] God will not give up on his dream for creation. The resurrection is the first statement of his final victory, and that victory is certain. Already we are living in its liberty.

The Power of "Yes"

Not only does Christ bring us the truth about living; he provides the strength and courage and, yes, the desire to deal with our shortcomings. Jesus didn't walk out of the tomb on Easter morning and then get a running start to see if we could catch him. Jesus understands what it is to be human. This understanding of our weakness is the beginning point of his dealing with us. Again, he loves us where he finds us, but he doesn't leave us there. His Spirit, the tangible experience of his risen life, lives with and in believers. The Spirit teaches, corrects, strengthens, and guides us daily. If we are weak in an area, the Spirit brings this to our attention. As we confess our weakness and accept our responsibility, the Spirit is faithful in helping us overcome our weakness.

Confession is not beating up ourselves for past mistakes, hoping that feeling bad about them will bring a catharsis for our sins. It's not a matter of wallowing in the hurt or telling Jesus anything he doesn't know already. What we are doing in confession is owning our actions. We are saying, "This is what happened. This is when I should have been brave but wasn't. This is when I should have turned away but didn't. This is my fault."

In his autobiography, noted pediatric surgeon Ben Carson wrote about having to deal with his temper as a young man. Once, when a friend threw a rock at him, he grabbed a bigger rock and threw it at the other boy's face, breaking his glasses and bloodying his nose.

A second incident was more extreme. When a friend changed the station on the radio they were listening to, the two got into a fight that ended when Carson pulled out a knife and tried to stab the other boy. He missed his friend's stomach only because he hit the boy's large belt buckle instead, breaking the blade of the knife. That made Carson realize he had a serious problem.

He retreated to the bathroom in his home and read his Bible and prayed that God would remove this terrible temper. He wrote, "Lord, despite what all the experts tell me, You can change me. You can free me forever from this destructive personality trait."[13] After spending almost all day in the bathroom, praying, reading Scriptures, crying, and begging God to help him, Carson finally found the peace he was searching for.

> At last I stood up, placed the Bible on the edge of the tub, and went to the sink. I washed my face and hands, straightened my clothes. I walked out of the bathroom a changed young man.

"My temper will never control me again," I told myself. "Never again. I'm free." And since that day, since those long hours wrestling with myself and crying out to God for help, I have never had a problem with my temper.[14]

This is only one story about one man, but the story can be repeated millions of times. When people are aware that true change is beyond their power and they call out to God, they find that he works in them to mold them more into the likeness of Christ. One of the most powerful arguments supporting the validity of the resurrection is that the disciples' lives were changed. How could Peter, who had denied even knowing Christ, be the same Simon Peter who later preached the message that ignited Pentecost? The religious leaders themselves realized that these men had been with Jesus.[15] And they *had* been with Jesus, not only during his earthly ministry, but also during his time on earth as the Risen Christ. Knowing Jesus was alive, resurrected from the dead, gave them the courage to confront the threats of the Sanhedrin.

THE HEALING BROUGHT ABOUT BY "YES"

As the Living Christ infuses every crevice and hidden place of believers' lives with his life, everything dark and broken is pushed out. His presence, alive in every Christ-follower, changes even our desires. As we follow Christ, we begin to pursue different things. We let go of the desires of our old lives and desire more of the things of Christ. I don't know how this happens; I just know it does. One day you will realize your tastes have changed. Peter stated it this way in his first letter: "now that you have tasted that the Lord is good."[16] Our tastes will have been ruined for anything else.

The resurrection of Jesus wasn't a grand magic trick to show how cool God is. The resurrection was part of his mission to find the lost, heal the sick, and bring the wanderers back home. Just as Christ was freed from death, so his followers have been set free. We are not only freed from the permanence of physical death, but we are free from all expressions of death as well. Believers in Christ live in eternity after their earthly lives end. And all forms of death in their lives, such as relationships ruined by anger and opportunities squandered by unbelief and disobedience, also are redeemed by the resurrection. The Risen Christ brings life to us not only for eternity but also for every minute of every day. He lives in us and through us so that none of his eternal purposes are lost or frustrated.

The Risen Christ is not limited by time and space, so he is with us in the present, and he waits for us in the future. He has secured the future, and our hope rests in him. Jesus taught his disciples to pray, "Thy kingdom come. Thy will be done in earth, as it is in heaven."[17] This was not an empty recitation or a righteous-sounding ritual. These words have meaning for us now as we live on earth. As we follow Jesus, we learn the ethics of heaven and begin to live them here, as best we can. We long for the day when swords will be beaten into plowshares and the wolf and the lamb will lie down together. We ache for the moment we will study war no more. Until then, we will practice heaven's ways right where we are.

This is how God's Kingdom comes to earth and how his will is done on earth. It is done in us. It is done through us.

THE ULTIMATE HOPE

Let's face it. If Jesus has not been raised from the dead, Christianity is over. If someday an archaeologist digs in a cave and finds Jesus's body, and if through the application of forensic science and the analysis of other evidence found in the tomb it is proved to be his body, then Christianity is over. If Christ is not alive, Christians have nothing else to say to the world.

Again, to quote Paul:

If there is no resurrection of the dead, then not even Christ has been raised. And if Christ has not been raised, our preaching is useless and so is your faith. More than that, we are then found to be false witnesses about God, for we have testified about God that he raised Christ from the dead. But he did not raise him if in fact the dead are not raised. For if the dead are not raised, then Christ has not been raised either. And if Christ has not been raised, your faith is futile; you are still in your sins. Then those also who have fallen asleep in Christ are lost. If only for this life we have hope in Christ, we are of all people most to be pitied.[18]

But we *do* have hope, because Christ is alive, and our testimony joins that of all Christ-followers since that first Easter. The world changed that Sunday morning. We were changed the moment the Risen Christ appeared to us. We stopped living for ourselves, and we started living for him. The resurrection is God's high-volume "yes," shouted to all his creation. "Watch," he says, "I am making everything new!"[19] When Jesus walked out of the tomb, God's "yes" was heard and continues to be heard—echoing off eternity.

The Mess Before the "Yes"

Who we used to be doesn't determine who we can become

Here is a trustworthy saying that deserves full acceptance:
Christ Jesus came into the world to save sinners—of whom
I am the worst.

—PAUL (1 TIMOTHY 1:15)

Whenever I talk about finding our "yes," people get excited. That's understandable, since God's plan for us is the best news we will ever hear. But then people remember something that stands out as a dark episode in their past. You can see the change in their countenances, as if someone had reached into their souls and turned off the light. One moment they are full of hope and possibilities, and the next, there's no hope at all.

Everyday life can feel as though you're running through an airport concourse trying to catch a flight. And no matter how hard you try or how fast you move, sometimes you arrive at the gate just as the plane is pulling away. Now you're stuck where you are with no way to reach your destination on time, or maybe ever. That is similar to the feeling people have when they first realize all the promise contained in God's "yes" *and then* remember something from their past. Have they missed their only chance to get where they had hoped to go in life? Did an action or choice they made years ago close the door just as the plane was pulling away from the gate, leaving them stranded where they are?

I can almost read those thoughts, without knowing the specifics of a person's life. We all have a past. Even though we find new life in Christ, no one starts from zero. Your life and mine, like any good story, have a prequel.

THE PAST IS NOT PAST

Every story has a story before the story you're reading. Moviemakers sometimes end a film in such a way that a sequel could follow if the first movie proves to be a box-office success. When the sequel possibilities are exhausted, producers invent the "prequel"—the story before the initial story.

People, like movies, have prequels. We all have lived a lot of life prior to the present moment. And sometimes our past has a way of living *into* the present. As William Faulkner reminds us, "The past is never dead. It isn't even past."[1] And if our lives are too full of pain, guilt, anger, and disappointment from the past, we may not have room for anything else, not even good things from God. Hands that still hold grudges can't be open to receive the future that Christ is trying to give us.

There is no question that parts of our past are painful. A lot of us have gone to great lengths to overcome mistakes and get beyond the kind of life we used to live. Most of us find a place of equilibrium—not a place of peace or joy, just a place where things are not too bad. Our past, we are sure, has robbed us of any chance of real happiness.

In the movie *Get Low*, Robert Duvall plays reclusive backwoodsman Felix Bush. Because he has had nothing to do with anyone for more than forty years, people have made up all kinds of stories about him. One day Felix comes to town and engages the services of the local mortuary to plan his funeral, but there is a catch. Felix wants to be there to hear what people have to say about him.

When the day of the funeral arrives, scores of people drive into the countryside to witness the spectacle. But Felix is in no mood to listen to the townspeople; instead, he tells the story of a love affair and the tragic accident that drove him into the woods so long ago.[2] Like Felix Bush, a lot of us have been hiding in self-imposed emotional exile, trying to pay for our real or imagined crimes. Our goal has often narrowed down to finding a life of little to no pain. But peace is much more than the absence of conflict, and joy is more than not being sad. Jesus came to offer a life of *more* to all of us, no matter what happened before.

YES...BUT

Whenever I talk to people about hearing God's "yes," they start to see the hope that lies in finally leaving behind their regrets and the pain caused by their mistakes, but... There's always a *but*.

Linguists have noted that this conjunction possesses an interesting power. Whenever the word *but* is used, people tend not to remember anything that was said before it. Your boss asks you to join him in his office late on a Friday afternoon. The conversation begins like this: "We have really appreciated your work for our company these last several years, *but*..." Later you don't remember anything from the conversation except that you were laid off. A young man receives a Dear John letter (or text) from his girlfriend that reads, "I have really enjoyed dating you for the last three months, *but*..." The young man remembers only one thing from the message: he was dumped. Hearing the word *but* removes everything before it from our memory.

For most of us, sin possesses the same kind of power. Sin is the great negation, the "no" that attempts to blot out the "yes" of Christ. Sure, Jesus loves you, *but* you're a sinner. After the *but* we forget everything else. How could Jesus love me when I'm a sinner? The memory of past sin and the realization of current sin loom large, blocking our view of the work Christ is doing in our lives today. Sin has a way of making us forget the goodness of God. Sin denies the presence and power of God in us and our world.

THE "NO" OF SIN

Sin tricks us into believing it has more power than it really does. At the same time, however, we often fail to follow the steps laid out by God to deal with the effects of sin in our lives. When we don't take advantage of confession *and* repentance, sin continues to hold us in its grip.

Christians are familiar with forgiveness. How many times have we heard preachers (and I am one) tell us, "Just confess your sin"? We emphasize that God's forgiveness is a free gift, there for the asking. But in emphasizing forgiveness, we inadvertently cheapen it. We skip over the necessity of repentance, which includes confession but goes beyond it to a definite change in how a person approaches life. God forgives us when we confess, but if we don't change at that point, leaving behind the sin that brought us to confession, we enter a revolving door.

People sin, then confess their sins, and go back and sin some more. This is not the gospel. When Jesus forgave the woman caught in adultery, he ended the conversation by telling her, "Go and sin no more."[3] Jesus's approach was not intolerant or judgmental; it was his way of helping the woman find healing and a new life. Repentance literally means "to change one's mind." It means that after confessing sin, the person turns from her previous lifestyle and commits to follow Christ. Without an emphasis on repentance, people keep on sinning and casually assume Jesus will always be there to forgive them. Holding such a cavalier attitude toward sin does untold damage in our lives.

What God has made, sin unmakes. What God has created, sin destroys. Where God left beauty, sin leaves scars.

In 1972 a disturbed man named Lazlo Toth took a hammer into a museum and attacked Michelangelo's *Pietà*. He chipped off several pieces of the famous statue, including Mary's nose. People wondered what would prompt someone to deliberately damage such a work of beauty. The sadness we feel over an act that defaced such a magnificent work of art gives us some insight into how the heart of God must break every time he sees one of us wounded by our mistakes and rebellion. Sin mars the image of God within us. We are the works of his hands[4] and the artwork in creation that most fully reflects the essence of the Artist.

THE FIRST STEP

In the story of the prodigal son, Luke uses a curious phrase when the younger son realizes what he has lost and determines to go home. The King James Version translates the phrase, "He came to himself."[5] That phrase has always fascinated me. How do you come to yourself? Can you set yourself down somewhere and then forget where you left yourself? Actually, it is something like that. We can become so buried under mistakes and failure, stuffed under grief and regret, that we get to the place where we no longer recognize ourselves. But God's "yes" changes all that. When the Spirit changes our true identity in Christ, we leave behind everything that is false and start walking toward the truth of Christ and who he created us to be.

Changing your mind

Walking away from the lies and destruction of sin is very close to the practical meaning of biblical repentance. It goes far beyond feeling bad about your sin—all the way to literally changing the direction of your life. And to change your life, you have to change the way you think. A change in your life's direction means you stop fighting the current of God's grace that flows in your spirit. Now you start flowing *with* the current of grace. As you reorient your life in the direction of God's leading, you find your efforts are amplified through the Spirit's presence in the same way an ocean current enhances the work of a ship's sails.

When we talk about Christian conversion, we emphasize feelings of conviction and a decision to confess our sins and seek forgiveness. But we don't stress the essential role played by our thinking. The problem that results is we don't change the way we think, so we end up not changing our behavior. For a total transformation of a person's life, the mind as well as the heart must change. We live the way we do because we think the way we do. The mess is in our heads before it is in our lives, but it moves from the mind to daily life.

This changes when we ask Christ to renew our minds, to alter the way we think. We need to allow our minds to be completely transformed. "Therefore, I urge you, brothers and sisters, in view of God's mercy, to offer your bodies as a living sacrifice, holy and pleasing to God—this is your true and proper worship."[6] When your mind is transformed, your life will follow.

I am not naive. I understand the lure of sin and the effectiveness of its deceptions. And I am familiar with the consequences of sin. I have sat with large numbers of people and listened as they recognized and talked through the harmful consequences of their actions. When the cost of their failures sinks in, it is devastating. A man's infidelity cost him his wife and children. For a few minutes of pleasure, he traded away a future with his family. It takes only one incident to disrupt a friendship, a career, a family, a life. Lies are told, discovered, and confessed in tears, but how can a person regain trust? Sin looks good in the moment but only because it's hiding the future consequences.

I'm convinced we don't understand the total impact of salvation. We make it about feelings or a one-time decision to confess our sins and trust in Christ's death and resurrection. But to live a new life, to be completely transformed, our salvation has to be about the total person, including our minds.

Changing your frame of reference

If in obedience to Christ we are going to make different choices, we have to adopt Christ's way of looking at things. God will create a new mind in you and me, but we have to join willingly in the process. And part of thinking differently is letting go of old assumptions and preferences and accepting the preferences of God.

In Acts 10 we read the story of the early church hearing from God a "yes" that led to its dropping of ethnic barriers. A Roman centurion named Cornelius was praying, and in his prayers he was told to find a man named Peter. Peter, in the meantime, also was praying. In his prayers Peter saw a vision of a sheet holding all kinds of animals—and they weren't kosher. Although Peter was told to kill and eat, he refused. Again the vision came, and again Peter refused to eat. Each time, Jesus confronted Peter with the following rebuke: "Do not call anything impure that God has made clean."[7] Only when Cornelius's messengers appeared at his gate did Peter begin to understand the message of the vision. Nothing created by God, people most of all, can ever be called unclean.

God created Gentiles just as he did Jews, and no one—Gentiles included—was inferior to anyone else. God loves those outside the nation of Israel on a par with the descendants of Abraham. Having grown up under the influence of Jewish traditions and biases, Peter must have had difficulty processing this. But to his credit, he was obedient to Christ and changed the way he thought about these matters. And not just the way he thought, but his life and his preaching as well.

Free of condemnation

There are two reasons we should not condemn others or ourselves. First, we all are created in the image of God. And second, Christ died for sinners. This is the price God was willing to pay for our redemption. We are called to live in the glory of knowing what we are worth. And when we don't, we damage ourselves, one another, and the world we live in. Sin devalues us as people and causes us to see others and all creation as lacking worth. Sin negates the good work Christ does in us and in the world. Where Christ speaks "yes," sin says "no."

We have things in our lives that cause shame or grief, and they act as a giant *but* to the good news of Christ. He promises us new life, which sounds great, but…"my family business went bankrupt after I misspent some accounts. I was going to pay it back, but then everything collapsed." And suddenly we forget the promise of Christ. He promises forgiveness and second chances, but it's hard to believe the second chance could still apply after the things we've done.

Why do we think that we alone committed a sin so horrible it exceeds Jesus's ability to forgive? This kind of thinking is the ultimate heresy. What we are saying is the death of Jesus was payment enough for everyone else's sins, but our sin is so monstrous that his death isn't enough to cover it.

Let Christ change the way you think so you can let go of that lie. Jesus paid it all. No part of the debt has been left for you or me to pay by working hard to clean up our own lives. On our own we can't get clean enough to impress God. Whatever we might try, we will always be unworthy of his love. The gift of God's "yes" in Christ is unearned, given to us freely. Our relationship with God is not a contract; it is a covenant, a bond of mutual love and commitment. In this covenant the parties are not equal, but the arrangement is mutual. Christ died for us and offers us his salvation, and we accept what he did for us as a free gift—on his terms.

Christ opens the door; we need only to walk through it. We then live our lives in loving response to God's grace expressed in Jesus. This is the mutual love and commitment of the covenant. Yet, for some reason, we have a hard time believing the gift of salvation is free. Who would give away something like that? So we think we have to earn it.

JUST START

In the South you will hear a curious expression. People will tell you they are "fixin' to get ready" to do something or to go somewhere. For instance, a friend might be "fixin' to get ready to go to the store." Notice, he isn't headed out to the store. He is not even getting ready to go the store.

He is fixin' to get ready to go. While this expression may be new to you, it carries a truth we're familiar with. We hear the good news of Jesus, and we are "fixin' to get ready" to believe, but first we need to change a few things. We want to straighten out some crooked places. *Then* we will get started on our journey with Jesus. But just when it seems we'd be ready, there is one more project to complete. We need to get everything fixed first, then we can get ready to go. Too many people spend their entire lives fixin' to get ready to follow Jesus.

Jesus is not unaware of the mess you are in, and he knows better than anyone that you can't fix it on your own. The mess you are in is why he came. And now that he is here, it makes no sense to waste any more time. So get started. Jesus will start wherever you are.

In the Christmas story, Mary and Joseph travel to Bethlehem and find there is no lodging available. They end up staying in a stable, and that is where Jesus is born. We make a big deal about this. "Sweet little Jesus boy," we sing, "born in a manger."[8] How could the world be so cruel as to make the Son of God be born in a stable? How could there be no room in the world for him? You have heard the sermons and songs that address this perceived injustice. I say "perceived" because the one Person who doesn't complain is God himself. A manger in a stable in Bethlehem may not have been much, but it was good place to start. Over and over in Scripture you see the same theme: things may not be perfect, but all God is looking for is a good place to start.

Jesus took challenges and difficulties in stride. A difficulty, after all, was no reason to change course. It was simply an opportunity to call on God for a solution in keeping with his "yes." Jesus had been preaching in the countryside, and five thousand men and their families were there listening but hadn't brought food. "How will we feed them?" asked some of the disciples. Well, what did they have to work with? A boy had a lunch consisting of two fish and five loaves of bread. "Great! Bring them to me," Jesus said.[9] It was a good place to start.

Jerusalem was a great city in the first seventy years of the first century.

Even though Israel was occupied by Rome, the capital city still attracted people from far beyond Judea. Jesus could have made this great city his base of operations, but instead he used a village known as Capernaum. It wasn't much of a place in the time of Jesus. It's not much now. But it was the place Jesus chose to start.

A woman came to a well in Samaria and found Jesus sitting there. Was he waiting for someone to draw water for him to drink, or was he waiting for a chance to speak with her? He opened her eyes to God and his truth. He told her that being a Samaritan—people despised in the eyes of the Jews—did not lessen God's love for her. He spoke to her without prejudice. Then Jesus told her about her life, and he didn't tell her to first get her life straightened out and then come back. He said, in effect, "This is who you are… This is what is going on right now in your life… And this is a good enough place to start."[10]

Starting seems to be the hardest part for us. How often have you thought that you need to begin a diet and exercise program but this week doesn't seem like the right time to begin? Most of us know at least three things that, if we did them, would immensely improve our lives. Maybe do a better job managing our money, or spend more time with our family, or decide once and for all if we're going to change careers, go back to school, or start a business. Information is rarely the problem. We just never get started.

Maybe the problem, as we discussed earlier, is the word *but*. A past failure could be blocking our vision, and since we tried once and failed, now it's easier not to try. Doing nothing seems the best way to avoid another failure.

There is always a cost associated with changing your life. To lose weight, you might have to give up some of your favorite foods and devote less time to social media so you can start exercising. You might have to rethink some of your relationships, and that's always tricky. Perhaps the price is too high. Whatever our reason, we fail to start so we never know authentic transformation. That's sad, because all Jesus really wants is a place to start.

When Jesus Said "Yes" to a Demon-Possessed Man

In one of Jesus's most famous miracles, he healed a man who had so many demons he felt like an entire army had invaded his life.[11] To me, this story illustrates our frustration with life in the frantic digital age. We feel as if we can't rest because something demands our attention 24/7. We are bombarded with too many voices, and they all tell us what is cool and what is not, what success looks like and what it doesn't...and these expectations change moment by moment. No one can keep up with it all. Like the demon-possessed man, we feel as if we have so many voices in our heads that our lives are unmanageable. You can, in fact, lose yourself in the noise and distraction.

This is why his healing is so important to us. When villagers came to check out what was going on, they found him fully clothed, sitting patiently, listening to Jesus. And here's the big point: he was in his right mind. There, in simple terms, is a way to understand the man's problem. He had been in his "wrong mind," which explains some things in our world. Wrong minds think up is down, love is hate, and hate is love. And once you get your mind wrong, how do you ever get it right again? If you can't trust the signals your mind is sending you, how do you find reality?

The problem is you can't. True change isn't about trying harder or working on a new plan. Until you can change your mind, anything you do will be filtered through a wrong mind. The gospel is bad news before it is good news, and the bad news is this: we are in a mess, and we can't fix it. We can only repent of being in our wrong minds. Too many of us have decided that repentance means to feel guilty for a little while and then say we are sorry. But apologizing is a long way from repenting.

The Greek word for "repentance" is *metanoia,* and it means to "change one's mind about something, to change one's perception about a given event or experience." Jesus, in his first sermon, preached, "Repent, for the kingdom of God is at hand."[12] Jesus calls for much more than a temporary feeling of guilt. He requires a radical transformation in light of new realities. What are the new realities? In Christ, the Kingdom of God—the very rule of God—has come close to us. God's Kingdom is close enough for us to jump in and join what he is doing, which requires a radical change of mind, a true *metanoia.* The Kingdom of God has come near in Christ, so we have to change our minds about love, truth, reality, eternity, Jesus, God, wealth, success, strength, weakness, hope, joy, and love. In other words, everything!

The "Yes" of Right Thinking

This is what Paul was talking about in Philippians 2 when he told the early church to "have the same mindset as Christ Jesus."[13] Jesus says we should love God with all our hearts, *minds,* and souls. To love God is to think in an entirely new way. We think of Jesus in a new way. We see and understand God in a new way as Jesus reveals the Father to us.

And we understand ourselves in a new way. This is probably one of the most overlooked aspects of salvation. No longer are we failures, but we are "chosen by God and precious to him."[14] While we may not be much by the world's standards, we have been purchased with an unmeasurable price, and knowing that, well, it changes the way we live. While all of us have a past, we need not be defined by it. We are not the victims of our hasty and unwise choices. Instead, the image of God defines us, and the price that Christ paid for us confirms our worth. Now we are called to live a new life in Christ. While the story of every human life begins in a prequel to the life we are now living, our faith calls us to live in the "yes" of Christ, which pulls us into his future victory. Our lives may begin with a mess, but they end with the Divine Yes.

The "Yes"
of Forgiving Others

*Forgiveness is how God deals with us
and how we deal with the world*

> Then Peter came to Jesus and asked, "Lord, how many
> times shall I forgive my brother or sister who sins against
> me? Up to seven times?" Jesus answered, "I tell you, not
> seven times, but seventy-seven times."
>
> —MATTHEW 18:21–22

It's easy to suspect that Peter was trying to get by with the bare minimum when he asked Jesus his famous question about forgiving others. But in Matthew 18, Peter was being generous in suggesting that he would offer forgiveness seven times. How many times would you or I forgive someone? Twice? Three times, maybe?

I can hear the conversation that would take place after a friend had wronged me for the fourth time. He comes to me, asking forgiveness. Now it's my turn to set him straight. "Forgive you? I can't believe you're even asking. I *already* forgave you three times!"

Given the natural inclination of the average believer, Peter's suggestion that we forgive someone seven times is, well, outrageous. And then Jesus ups the ante. He doesn't think Peter is being generous enough. Instead of seven times, Jesus said, forgive seventy-seven times! Who can forgive that many times? Who could even keep track of that many acts of forgiveness while being upset over a person's repeated hurtful behavior? Well, that's the point. We aren't supposed to keep track. Just keep forgiving.

But why set the bar so high? Because Jesus knows that unless we come to a place where we forgive those who have wounded us, we're stuck. Forgiveness is how we get unstuck. Anger, left unattended, becomes bitterness. Grudges, carefully nursed over the years, produce a hard heart. Our pain blinds us to the needs of those around us and isolates us from others.

In order to receive the new life Christ is offering, you first have to let go of the old one. Forgiveness is how you do that.

It's Yours to Deal With

Sometimes the cause of all the turmoil was not your fault. You were betrayed, wounded, lied to. You felt as though you were left alone in your pain. But in God's "yes" you have more options than you realize.

The first thing to do—and this is crucial—is to accept responsibility for dealing with your pain. Whether it was self-inflicted or completely undeserved, it is yours to deal with. In fact, you will end up dealing with the pain and anger one way or another—either intentionally in a constructive way or in some other way that will eat at you. You might try to avoid it or deny it. You can try to hide your anger. But doing so can lead to health problems, depression, and any number of addictions—alcohol, drugs, food, possessions, work, or sex. Addictions have no power to rid you of pain, and instead they bring added problems.

Or you could choose a life of perpetual victimhood. That way you feel justified in blaming your failures on the injustice that was done to you. In the movie *On the Waterfront,* Marlon Brando's character realizes he has been betrayed and blurts out, "I coulda been a contender!"[1] A lot of us have used that line or a sentiment similar to it. We feel that our lives would have been different if our fathers had been emotionally present, if our mothers had stood by us, if our spouses had not betrayed us, or if our friends had not abandoned us. (Feel free to add your own story here.) If others had acted differently, then our lives would have turned out differently. But instead of receiving the gift of a good life, we feel we are forever crippled by what someone else did.

When you live with that attitude, you are becoming a victim a second time—now by your own choice. Victimhood is self-inflicted pain, and you need to reject it. Take responsibility for your anger, and deal with it in a redemptive manner. Until you decide to take this step, you can't move forward.

MOE FOR A DAY

I understand why you might feel as if getting revenge is the only fair way to deal with someone who hurt you. But it's a lot like the Three Stooges. There's a bit where Moe slaps Larry, and Larry slaps Curly, but then Curly doesn't have anybody to slap. Don't you wish, just for one day, you could be Moe and walk around slapping every person who needs to be slapped?

Let's say I could crown you Moe for a Day. Now you're authorized to slap anyone you've wanted to slap and without fear of retribution. You won't be slapped back. And no one will think less of you, because they expect this sort of thing from Moe. Remember, today you're Moe, so think about who you'd slap. (Whenever I tell this story, everyone has a list ready.)

If you went out and started slapping people, you would discover two hard realities. First, making someone else hurt doesn't take away your pain. You can never make yourself feel better by making someone else feel worse. Second, you would do what all of us would do. You would slap a person one too many times. And once you wronged the other person, *he* would become Moe, and he could slap you back. The two of you would stand there slapping each other, like two stooges, until it wasn't funny anymore.

You need to deal with your hurt and anger, but let go of the idea that hurting the person who hurt you will do any good. The first step toward healing is realizing that the pain belongs to you alone. No one else can solve it. So own it, and then you can start dealing with it.

New Realities Open New Futures

Two great realities can open up a new future. The first is this: God is not limited by space and time. He can be anywhere anytime, and he is everywhere all the time. Sometimes when you focus on trying to fathom God, your eyes cross and you feel dizzy. When I consider that God slides across the space-time continuum without constraint, being both here and there, arriving somewhere else before he left where he was, I have to take a rest and think about something else. I can't process it all.

The truth that God transcends all limits other than those he imposes on himself is not just an interesting topic to discuss. It is critical to our drawing on his help and his power in addressing our struggles. Here's why: God is waiting for you in your future and for me in my future. We don't deal with our hurts and struggles in vain. We have hope for what lies ahead because Christ is there waiting for us. He has already completed the future and is there for us before we arrive.

At the same time, he is with us in our present. And he is in our past, all at the same time. This is when God being God makes a lot of difference to us on a practical level. God is free to go to that spot where the worst thing that ever happened to you occurred, to the moment when your soul was cut in half. God is there in your past, and he can heal the past right now so it will no longer bleed into the present.

The second great truth is that God is always working, and because God is always working, he has the power and mercy to adapt for our good the changing circumstances caused by our choices as well as the actions and decisions of other people that affect us. Leslie Weatherhead was pastor of City Temple in London, England, during World War II. As you can imagine, the suffering of the war gave rise to questions about good, evil, suffering, and God. To respond to some of the questions, Dr. Weatherhead gave a series of lectures, which were later published in his book *The Will of God.*[2] He presented three categories to help readers understand how God works in the world: the intentional will, the circumstantial will, and the ultimate will.

God began with an intention. He placed Adam and Eve in the garden with the intent that they would be happy forever. They disobeyed God's one prohibition and were thrown out of the garden, so God adapted his intentional will to the new circumstance. Now he was working within his circumstantial will. All the while, Weatherhead points out, God was working through every circumstance to bring about his ultimate will. He continues to work that way today.

Our confidence and hope are not based on having the courage to do the right thing; they are based on God and his character. If we had to depend on our own courage to always do the right thing, we'd fall into despair. No one is that consistent or dependable. But God is always strong and good, and he will not be defeated in his redemptive work. Ever.

You are not defined by your anger, hurt, or sense of being a victim. God is the only One who can define you. That means your future need not be held hostage to your past. There is another choice, God's choice, which is forgiveness.

FORGIVENESS, THEN RESTORATION

You're right. I don't understand how badly you were hurt. No one can fully understand another person's pain. Even if we've had similar hurts, we will experience them differently. Yet while each experience is unique, there is a commonality that binds us together. All of us understand what it is to be hurt. And all of us understand the difficulty of forgiveness.

But difficult or not, we need to take advantage of the power of forgiveness and to seek restoration. Forgiveness and restoration are two different realities. Forgiveness is necessarily a part of restoration, but restoration may or may not be part of forgiveness. Indeed, in some situations attempting restoration with the offending party would be unwise and unsafe. Paul said, "As much as it is up to us, we should live in peace with all people."[3] In qualifying his statement, Paul was acknowledging that it's not always possible to achieve peace with another person. Forgiveness is extended by one person, and the other party may or may not accept it. But restoration always requires the involvement of both parties.

Yet the prospect of an unresponsive second party does not release you from the requirement to forgive that person. Forgiving her is more for your benefit than for hers. It's counterintuitive, I know, because forgiving the wrongdoer seems unfair to you, the wronged party. But, in truth, when you forgive someone, you are then set free from bondage to the desire for revenge. Forgiveness is unilateral, so you'll reap the benefits whether the other person responds or not. And hopefully it will bless both of you, bringing some healing to the wrongdoer as well. In many cases there is restoration.

Forgiving could be the hardest thing you've ever done, depending on what was done to hurt you. But I know that people are able to forgive even things that seem unforgivable. In October 2006 a lone gunman entered a small school in the Amish community of Nickel Mines, Pennsylvania. After holding some of the students hostage, he shot ten girls, killing five, and then committed suicide. To the amazement of the world, the Amish families forgave the gunman. They even attended his funeral, understanding that his mother had lost a son.[4] The community refused to allow this tragedy to define them. They would not be held prisoner to anger, trapped in a never-ending cycle of recalling the horrid details of the past.

I don't understand your pain, just as I can't imagine the suffering of the parents who lost children in that shooting. But I do know this: until you find a way to forgive, whoever wounded you will hold you hostage.

MODELS OF FORGIVENESS

The most famous story of forgiveness is captured in Jesus's act of forgiving those who crucified him. "Father, forgive them," Jesus prayed, "for they do not know what they are doing."[5] Even as Jesus was dying, he was releasing his tormentors from responsibility for his death. How could Jesus, in the midst of unimaginable pain, manage to keep his thoughts about him enough to pray that his executioners be forgiven? Again, the love of God is bigger than we can know—big enough even to reach out from the cross to a lost world that was at that moment putting him to death.

Okay, you say, but that was Jesus. What about a mere human who has real-life hurts inflicted by members of his own family? Well, we have the story of a son with an overprotective father and vengeful, bullying brothers. The brothers stripped off the boy's clothes and left him in a hole to die. Then, finding an even better way to make Joseph suffer, the brothers sold him to slave traders and told their father that he had been killed. Think about it: you are hated by your brothers, beaten and left to die, then sold into slavery, and given up as dead. Yet this man, Joseph, found a way to forgive.

As we watch Joseph negotiate the obstacles that life throws at him, it is a lesson in how to live out Paul's teaching to be content in every situation. Joseph went from a privileged childhood (his father wouldn't even let him do chores) to being sold into slavery and then thrown into prison for a crime he didn't commit. But eventually he was elevated to the rank of Pharaoh's most trusted advisor. I encourage you to spend some time with Joseph's story.[6]

Joseph was serving as Pharaoh's advisor and had stockpiled grain in advance of a famine that would affect the entire known world. Egypt became the grocery store to the world and as a result was becoming a wealthy nation. Everybody had to come to Egypt to buy food—everybody, including Joseph's family.

One day as he was overseeing the distribution of food, he recognized his brothers standing in line. By that time Joseph looked Egyptian, and his brothers didn't recognize him. They couldn't understand his language, but he understood theirs. Joseph could barely hold himself together, but he managed not to give anything away.

While he wanted to tell them who he was, he couldn't bring himself to trust his brothers. His solution was to put them through a series of tests. Had they changed since selling him into slavery? When he was satisfied they were not the same bullies as before, he told them who he was. Now they feared the tables had been turned. They were afraid Joseph would have them killed, but he didn't. He forgave them.

In one of the most profound moments in the Bible, Joseph told his brothers, "You intended to harm me, but God intended it for good."[7] Joseph was able to see the work of God in his life, including the moments that were meant to destroy him.

God used slavery to get Joseph into Egypt. Once there, God used the prison experience to get Joseph connected to people who would put him next to Pharaoh. Every time Joseph thought he had reached the end, God presented another opportunity. There was nothing good about what happened to Joseph. Sold into slavery, falsely imprisoned, and forgotten by friends—this sounds like a tragic story on *Oprah*. But God used all of it to bring about a series of circumstances for protecting his chosen people.

And for our immediate purposes, Joseph's story provides a number of keys in understanding forgiveness.

First, even though Joseph was going through undeservedly tough times, he never gave in to despair. I am sure working as a slave in Potiphar's house, then serving time in prison for a crime he didn't commit, and then being forgotten in prison gave him plenty of reasons to throw in the towel. If I were in the same situation, I would not only give up, but I would also give in to my anger and try to get even with everyone who hurt me. But Joseph was always aware that his choices mattered, even how he acted toward other prisoners. He was always faithful to God regardless of how unfaithful or deceitful others were to him.

Second, Joseph worked hard to keep his relationship with God vital and deep. The language of dreams is a deep language of the soul and can only be heard in a very quiet life. I don't understand how he maintained such a quiet spiritual life in the midst of the chaos he was going through, but he did. Too many times we allow the noise of our anger and the sulking of our grudges to deafen us to God's word to us. Joseph's emotional breakdown when he recognized his brothers shows how much he had been hurting during his separation from his family. Yet he didn't allow his pain and anger to separate him from God.

When we are wounded, we can give in to the pain, use our victimhood status as an excuse to act out, and try to wound others. By doing so, we then become the aggressor, the perpetrator of more violence. One of the things that makes following Jesus so difficult is that we are never given permission to disobey, regardless of the circumstances. We can't get away with saying, "Yes, I know I shouldn't have lost my temper, but you should have seen what the other guy did." Joseph maintained his obedience to God in spite of suffering extreme injustice.

Third, Joseph understood that forgiveness was the only way to stop the violence. If he had exacted revenge, the cycle of hatred would have started all over again. Pain would have given birth to more pain, which would have brought more and more pain. But forgiveness overwhelmed the earlier evil that had been done by his brothers. When Joseph forgave his brothers, there was nothing for them to fight against, nothing to resist. The energy that had once been used to hurt was now used by Joseph to heal. I guess the brothers could have stormed out in anger, but what would their justification have been? They didn't want to be forgiven? They didn't want their father to experience the joy of seeing his son again?

In recent times no one has portrayed the power of forgiveness more poignantly than Nelson Mandela and bishop Desmond Tutu of South Africa. After spending most of his life in prison before bringing down apartheid, Mandela had every reason to be angry. No one would have blamed him if he had demanded punishment for the deposed white rulers. He didn't. He extended forgiveness. Moreover, he demanded that the people of South Africa follow his example. With the help of Bishop Tutu, the South Africans set up Truth Councils, where the truth was sought, investigated, and announced. The guilty ones were forgiven by the people they had wronged. Without forgiveness, South Africa would not have survived as a nation. And without forgiveness, we won't survive either.

Lastly, Joseph always kept the big picture in mind. God was working in ways Joseph could not understand. God was accomplishing purposes that Joseph could not yet see. If Joseph had given in to the anger, he would have disqualified himself from the future that God was beginning to unfold. Paul wrote about living in such a way that we do not disqualify ourselves from winning the race we are running.[8] Joseph didn't lose sight of the fact that God was up to something.

In the push and shove of everyday life, it's hard to stay aware of how much God is working in the world around us. But, as Paul reminds us, being shortsighted and holding anger in our hearts gives Satan a foothold in our lives[9] and thus blocks us from being part of what God is up to. Because of Joseph's forgiveness, the future of Israel was secured. He knew God was working and didn't let his personal pain numb him to that ultimate reality.

Forgiveness Deals with Pain

Hearing God's "yes" means we trust God to be at work even when we can't see any obvious evidence of it. In fact, we are not only confident of his working, but we are also confident he is working for our good. We often quote Romans 8:28 but don't really take the time to understand it. "All things work together for good," Paul wrote.[10] Most of us are naive about this text, believing it promises that bad things will never happen to us. But the truth is just the opposite. Paul was confirming that bad things do happen, a reality the apostle knew as well as anyone. Read his letters and see how many times he was betrayed, disappointed, and abandoned by friends.

But here is the good news. Our God is so good and so powerful he can produce good out of even the worst things people do to us. God can so transform the harm that was intended that we will give thanks for how he used our wounds for his work. Joseph, betrayed and sold into slavery, became the second-most-powerful man in Egypt and was able to save his family. Yet he would not have been in that good position if he had not been sold to slave traders.

Joseph always remembered he was a little part of God's big picture. And God's big "yes" to him trumped the "no" that resounded from his brothers.

In the power of God's "yes" to us in Jesus, we are not victims of our past or the effects of someone else's mistakes. We are given a choice. We can choose to be marked permanently by our wounds, or we can choose to be defined by the resurrection of Christ. I don't do it perfectly, but as much as I can, I choose to define my life by the resurrection.

FORGIVING AGAIN AND AGAIN

Forgiveness is more than a one-time thing. More often than not, the matter that we forgive will come up again. This frustrates us because we think we have dealt with it, and now we have to deal with it once more. The deeper the hurt, the more times we will have to deal with it.

We want forgiveness to be a stairstep. We deal with it, step up, and move on. But forgiveness may actually be more like a spiral staircase. You forgive as much as you can in the moment, and then you come back to the issue at a different level. Same stairway, and you're still on it. *But didn't I forgive this already?* Yes, as much as you could, but not at this level. Now you will deal with the issue at a more significant level and move on again. Like a spiral staircase, you are making progress. It just feels as though you are walking around in circles.

I have a friend who grew up with an alcoholic father. The pain of his childhood was more than anyone should have to bear. When he was talking to me about his early life, I could still feel the heat of his anger, and more than once I could see it in his tears.

I asked my friend what he heard from Jesus whenever he prayed for his drunken father. I could tell by his shocked look that he had never thought to pray for his father. He wouldn't even let the idea cross his mind.

"You know," I went on, "Jesus says to pray for your enemies and those who hurt you."

"I'm not going to pray for my father."

"You have to."

"No I don't," he said. "I hate him."

"I know you do. That's why you have to pray for him."

"I won't do it," he insisted. "My dad is off-limits."

"Think about it," I said. "Sooner or later you'll have to deal with it."

I didn't see my friend for several weeks. When I did, he told me he had started praying for his dad. Surprised, I asked what had happened.

"Nothing," he said. "Nothing happened for a long time. Then one day when I was praying, I felt a strong need to forgive my dad. I didn't want to, but I knew I had to. It's like Jesus told me I could hold on to the anger or I could hold on to him, but I couldn't do both."

That's it. You can hold on to your anger, or you can hold on to Jesus, but you can't hold on to both. Forgiveness is how we let go of anger and hurt to get a firm hold on the "yes" of God offered to us in Jesus Christ. Forgiveness is releasing the person who hurt you from the expectation that he could ever fix the harm he did to you. He can't. Once you have been wounded, only Christ can heal you. He does that by first giving you the grace to forgive those who wronged you. As my friend found out, you can hold only so much in your heart. You must choose either the "yes" of Christ or the "no" of refusing to forgive. If you choose "no," you will be tied to the anger of unforgiveness.

I am praying you will choose God's "yes" of forgiveness.

Surprised by "Yes"

Finding the treasure
you already have

> For no matter how many promises God has made, they
> are "Yes" in Christ. And so through him the "Amen" is
> spoken by us to the glory of God.
>
> —PAUL (2 CORINTHIANS 1:20)

Have you ever been lost? Really lost? Driving around in circles, trying to find a landmark that you recognize so you can get your bearings and find your way? You keep at it, but nothing looks familiar.

You don't know how you got to where you are, and you don't know how to get back to where you started. So you call the friend you were supposed to meet and tell her you're going to be late because you're lost. What does your friend say? "Where are you?" After the momentary frustration of being asked such a silly question, you start describing the unfamiliar landmarks you see around you. With any luck your friend will say, "I know where you are. Stay there, and I'll come get you."

The existential problem of humanity is that we are lost in the universe. We don't know where we are or how we got here. We certainly don't know how to get to God. But the good news of the gospel is not that you can get to God but that, in Christ, God has come to you. In the Incarnation, God said, "Stay where you are. I'll come to you." (And he doesn't leave us where he finds us, but that is another story. Right now, we're focusing on the overwhelming reality of knowing that God is searching for us.)

Life starts when God finds us. The gospel message isn't "Do these ten things, and you can get to God." The gospel message is "The Shepherd is still looking for his lost sheep." The gospel is not about being lost but being found. The "yes" of God is already in us, but only the light of his presence allows us to see it.

The World and Your Identity

The world has it backward. The world says it's up to you to hunt for things of value, which are buried in some far-off, unreachable location. You could spend a lifetime searching and still never uncover the things of lasting value. Who do you know that has been successful in this search? Anyone? This is why most of us find our heroes in stories rather than in real life.

You've heard the stories just as I have. A hero is forced to go on a great adventure, a daunting quest. Our hero has to leave his community and be tested in the wilderness. There are mountains to climb, deadly rivers to cross, evil trolls barring entrance to the next phase of the quest unless the hero solves an impossible riddle. Our hero has to overcome every threat, and the threats grow more dire the further our hero progresses. Finally he reaches the place where he can test his mettle against magical beasts that can be defeated only by secret knowledge!

If our hero survives all this, he will be rewarded with the knowledge of his true identity. (Don't forget, he is the humble son of starving peasants.) Now, however, he will be told that he is, in fact, the long-abandoned son of the gods. Finally he knows his destiny, the great purpose for which he was born. The fearsome journey through deadly terrain and past evil enemies has shaped the hero for the rest of his life. Any future success will result from lessons learned on this early pilgrimage of identity.

I don't know why the world wants us to believe that finding our identity is a near-impossible task, something so demanding that only the most revered heroes can achieve it. The world seems to be afraid that if we discover our true identity, we will live very differently. To keep that from happening, the world does all it can to keep our lives as busy and complicated as possible. If we spend our days and nights amid noise and stress, there never will be a quiet moment when the Spirit may whisper into the deep hunger of our lives.

The grand thoughts we had, as young men and women, about how we were going to change the world get lost under the mounting demands of mortgage payments and utility bills, work and family responsibilities, tragedy and disaster. The constant clanging of the urgent in our ears drowns out the quiet whispers of the important. Most of us never find time to seek answers to the great questions of life. That is, until we are old and look back on our lives and think, like the priest in Graham Greene's novel *The Power and the Glory,*

> We were just minutes from an appointment and that life could
> have easily been so much better had he made the simple choice
> to be a saint. For in the end, the priest finally discovers, the
> only thing that mattered was to be a saint.[1]

THE CHRISTIAN JOURNEY IS DIFFERENT

While the world demands that you go on a pilgrimage to find your destiny, the faith pilgrimage begins with God's declaration of who you really are and why he made you. The rest of your life is a journey that is given meaning and direction by God's determination of your identity and destiny.

Here is what makes this interesting. You don't have to prove yourself first by completing a test of endurance, courage, and skill. There is no rite of passage that qualifies you to follow God. It's just the opposite. God gives you his "yes" before you have shown any promise or early qualifications for the task. He goes ahead and calls you to join him in his divine work, and as you encounter him, God reveals your identity.

Richard Rohr, the highly regarded Catholic writer on spirituality, said, "It is as though we are all suffering from a giant case of amnesia."[2] He's right. We don't know who we are until Jesus tells us. This is where the terminology often used by Christians is not helpful. We do not "find Jesus." Jesus is not lost. We are. Jesus finds us, and in this finding, everything changes. Everything changes because we change. In our encounter with Christ, we find out who we are, and we understand the divine purpose to which we are called. God sees in us what we fail to see in ourselves, and he entrusts us to be part of his redemptive work.

Abraham and Sarah were called to leave their families and go to a land God was preparing for them. They had been told they would become the patriarch and matriarch of a great nation. There was just one problem. They didn't have any children. How can you be the parents of a great nation if you can't even get pregnant with your first child? Both were far beyond the age when children could be considered possible. If they ever had a child, it would be a miracle...and so it was.[3]

Remember Moses? What was it about Moses that made God choose him? Whatever it was, Moses didn't know himself. He wasn't an eloquent public speaker. Nothing in his past would make anyone think he was going to be one of the most famous men in history. He was born to a slave and hidden in a woven basket left floating in a river. He later became famous for being a good friend of God, but he spent forty years following sheep around. And they weren't even his sheep. No one on earth saw anything special in Moses. But God did.[4]

Gideon was hiding in a hole, trying to thresh wheat without being discovered by the hostile Midianites all around him. If a roving band had seen Gideon, they would have stolen his wheat and most likely killed him. Gideon lacked courage, but an angel who approached him didn't see him that way. The angel greeted Gideon with these words: "The

LORD is with you, mighty warrior." Gideon tried to help the angel understand there had been a mistake. He was far from a "mighty warrior."[5] Indeed, he was the runt of Israel, the smallest man in the smallest tribe. Talk about an unlikely leader. If the Israelites were headed into battle against the Midianites, who in their right minds would ask Gideon to lead them?

Everything Gideon said about himself was accurate. Everyone knew Gideon couldn't figure out how to raise an army and then devise a plan to defeat the Midianites. If any part of the operation succeeded, it would have to be a work of God. On a number of occasions, God had to give Gideon a sign to confirm he had indeed called Gideon to lead this battle. With him at the helm, everyone would know God was doing it. Still, God saw in Gideon something no one else could see.[6]

When Samuel was told to anoint the next king of Israel to take over the crumbling kingdom of Saul, he went to the home of Jesse, as commanded. Jesse was eager to show Samuel all his sons, but when the prophet didn't see the new king among any of the impressive young men, he asked Jesse if he had another son. In that moment Jesse remembered David, who was tending sheep. How is it that a father had to be reminded he had another son? In Jesse's eyes David lacked any qualities that would set him apart as a king.[7] Whatever was in David, God was the only One who saw it.

There was nothing about Mary, a teenage girl in Nazareth, that would mark her as the one who would give birth to God's Son. Yet the angel told her that God had been watching, and among all the women in the world, she was most blessed.[8] Only in the trials of being the mother of Jesus did she reveal the inner strength and dogged faith in God that had been unnoticed by those who knew her.

I wonder if any of the other disciples laughed out loud when Jesus called Peter "the Rock"? Surely those who had been with Peter would have recognized that the name just didn't fit. Perhaps, as is the case with some great leaders, this new nickname was aspirational. That is, Jesus gave Simon the name *Peter* with the idea that Simon would grow into the name. Those who follow church history may debate how close this apostle came to showing that he was, in fact, the Rock. But no one can deny that Peter became a major leader in the early church.[9]

Peter preached the sermon at Pentecost. Peter, along with John, led the early church in Jerusalem and was bold and steady under pressure exerted by local religious leaders. If tradition is correct, Peter became the undisputed leader of the church in the Roman Empire as bishop of Rome. There was something in Peter, and Jesus alone could see it.

After his conversion on the Damascus Road, Paul, then known as Saul, didn't know what to do. He was visited by a prophet named Ananias, who told Saul that Christ had set him, Saul, apart for a unique mission—carrying the gospel of the Jewish Messiah to the Gentiles of the world. Paul did not go along with this offer because of any promises of fame, success, or a life of ease. Instead, he would be imprisoned, beaten, stoned, whipped, shipwrecked, and left for dead.[10] Ananias had been obedient to God and found Saul—blind and confused—in a house in Damascus. Ananias, while doing what he had been told to do, must have wondered if there was some mistake. Saul showed none of the promise or potential that Ananias must have anticipated. Everything the prophet said about Paul's future service to God was not yet evident.[11]

And that is how God works. The "yes" is always about the future. Sitting in the house on Straight Street, wiping the scales from his eyes, Paul could have never understood the impact of his future ministry—preaching, establishing churches, confronting the Jerusalem church on its ethnic bigotry, and writing letters about faith and practice that we are reading two thousand years later. All that was yet to come. Jesus had seen in Paul something no one else had seen. The calling of Paul was lived out just as Jesus had predicted it would be.

The same is true for each of us. Jesus names his followers, and we spend the rest of our lives growing into the fullness of his vision for our identity and our destiny.

THE BLESSING OF THE COMMUNITY

The call is issued, an identity and destiny are revealed, and then the adventure begins. Each time, the journey validates the call, but the call comes first. The call is a gift, and in that gift we find our identity and destiny. Each step and obstacle in life are used to clarify and validate the purpose for which we were created.

New believers need to be told about this. If Christ is indeed making all things new, then people who are beginning to follow Christ need to be affirmed in their new identity. The early church emphasized connection to the community. Young believers were joined to mature believers to do life together. In everyday moments the faith would be taught, questions answered, and a destiny revealed. Any behavior that didn't meet the community's understanding of Christ would be corrected, and a new and better way taught. The process of discipleship was natural, following the ordinary events and experiences of everyday life, when the challenges of living a life faithful to Christ in a pagan world could be discussed. Under the watchful eye of a Christian mentor, the new convert's destiny would be called out through the revelation of the person's gifts and personality.

Too often the church today leaves new believers with nothing more useful than "Don't do what you used to do." In reality, being born again means just that—being born again, which means you have to learn to walk again, think again, speak again...everything again. And trying to do this on your own is just about impossible. No one lives the Christian life alone. It's too hard. We need one another on this journey. Believers need other believers to encourage us, confront us when necessary, and to remind us of both *who* we are and *whose* we are. Even the Lone Ranger had Tonto.

Which brings us to a second point. If your "yes" is found in an encounter with Jesus Christ, your "yes" is always confirmed in a Christ-following community. This is an important way for us to be sure the "yes" is actually from God and not a result of our own desires. As we discussed earlier, Ananias announced Paul's calling, but the church in Antioch confirmed that God had indeed called Paul. Barnabas was sent from Jerusalem to check on the new church at Antioch. When he realized the church needed a pastor, he went to get Paul. After he had been teaching at the church, the Spirit called Paul and Barnabas as the church's first missionaries. Paul's ministry was confirmed and supported by the local community that had witnessed the authenticity of Paul's teaching.[12] For each of us, community is vital to our hearing and recognizing the "yes" we feel God is speaking to us. Trying to live a solo Christian life leaves us too vulnerable to weaknesses of our own intelligence and spiritual maturity. We need brothers and sisters who will pray for us, grieve with us, hold us accountable, and, yes, celebrate with us.

THE BLESSING

Sadly, in both the church culture and the secular world, we have lost the power that used to accompany the word *blessing*. In biblical stories, such as the lives of Jacob and Esau, fortunes were found and lost according to the blessing. In their book *The Blessing*, John Trent and Gary Smalley help us recapture the potentially life-changing impact of the blessing.[13]

For most of us, *blessing* has become a throwaway word. But in the Bible, *blessing* meant the difference between success and failure, between fulfilling dreams or leaving them unrealized. And sometimes *blessing* meant the difference between life and death. To be blessed was to have your personality, your family life, and your professional life all empowered by the Spirit of God. In this way your actions were leveraged to their maximum potential. The poor farmer in the stories of Jesus could expect a return on his plantings of only three or four times what he planted. But Jesus told stories of harvesting thirty, sixty, even a hundred times more than what was planted. That's the power of blessing.

In Paul's case, Jesus told Ananias to lay hands on Saul and pray for him. The prophet was to tell Paul about the value Christ had placed on him and the future his ministry would have. Christ, through his Spirit, would accompany and empower Paul and his ministry in ways the apostle would marvel at years later. The life that Ananias prophesied for Paul did come true, in ways Paul would have never been able to see on his own. He had to have the community not only to see the vision but also to accomplish it.

And that still happens in the contemporary church.

THE STORY OF SWEET SLEEP

Jen Gash was the executive assistant to Bill Purcell, the mayor of Nashville, Tennessee. After moving to Nashville, she completed her degree at Middle Tennessee State University and entered the world of city politics. Everything was going well. She didn't see her position as being a career since sooner or later her boss would have to leave office and a new mayor would bring in his or her own team. There was a lot of energy and excitement to the job, and she was making some key connections for the future. She had developed a reputation as a hardworking, trustworthy, "get it done" kind of employee. After her stint at city hall, she would have been able to find any number of jobs. Then she went on a mission trip.

The funny thing is, Jen went on the trip without thinking too much about it. A friend asked her to go work with orphans in Moldova, the poorest of all the former Soviet-bloc nations. Jen loved children, and it seemed as if it would be fun. She was not prepared for what she encountered.

The mission team was working with orphans who, for beds, had nothing more than ragged, stained mattresses on rusted springs. Their clothes were hand-me-downs or what the orphans could scrounge for themselves. Feeding them healthy meals was even more difficult than clothing them. The problems were not caused primarily by corruption or intentional evil, though there was some of that. The problem was simply a lack of resources to take care of all the Moldovan orphans. And even if the youth could manage to leave the orphanage, they had little hope of improving their lives. Most of them would be lost to a life in criminal gangs or the European sex trade.

Jen knew something had to be done. What she wasn't prepared for was a growing awareness that God was calling her to be the one to do it. The reality that some child in the world was going to sleep without a decent bed was not something Jen was willing to tolerate. There had to be a way to do something about it. She established Sweet Sleep, a ministry dedicated to providing beds to the world's orphaned and abandoned children, demonstrating God's love for them and improving their quality of life. Okay, she would begin with Moldova, but make no mistake—her goal was and is to change the life of every orphan in the world.[14]

Using her administrative skills and contacts with leaders of every kind in Middle Tennessee (including this author and pastor), Jen was determined to garner the resources of churches and people of goodwill to provide beds, bedding, clothing, and life skills for orphans. Working with carpenters, she designed a bed that could be built for seventy-five dollars. The beds were simple in their construction and could be mass-produced by any woodworking shop in the world. People were asked to buy at least one bed each, and when enough beds were purchased, Jen and a team would head to Moldova to build them. In Moldova, she worked with churches, government agencies, craftsmen, and anyone else who would listen in order to get the beds built. Her trips soon expanded their reach to provide clothing, Bible studies, counseling, and missionary training. And eventually she was able to hire staff to operate this ministry in country.

Jen realized if she taught boys to build the beds, they could learn carpentry skills. If girls were taught to sew as a way to take care of clothing and bedding needs, they would learn a skill as well. What began as a need to get a child a bed was now a comprehensive orphan ministry. Soon invitations followed for Sweet Sleep to work in Uganda and other nations in Africa and then in Haiti. Because of Jen's reputation and her contacts in Haiti before the earthquake of 2010, she was able to get precious resources through the logjams and red tape that held up many other relief and development resources. Sweet Sleep is now an internationally recognized ministry, and Jen Gash is its president. All of it started in the heart of a mayor's executive assistant in Nashville, Tennessee.

First the Call, Then the Journey

First comes the call, then the gift, then the journey. This is one of the most difficult parts of God's "yes" for us to grasp. We keep thinking we have to do something to earn a new identity, a new calling, and a destiny in Christ. But the grace of God doesn't work on merit. Your identity, your destiny, is simply given to you. Your only response is to humbly receive the gift. Paul reminds us in Ephesians, "For it is by grace you have been saved, through faith—and this is not from yourselves, it is the gift of God—not by works, so that no one can boast."[15] Because you cannot earn God's grace, you may be tempted to feel like it's not really yours. It's as if someone is going to figure out that you have no legitimate claim to your "yes" and will take it away.

But let's look at it another way. One of the best gifts a child can give a parent is to enjoy the gifts the parent gives the child. Knowing your child is playing with the new doll or catcher's mitt or, better yet, giving the toy honor by putting it on a shelf when finished playing with it brings untold joy to any parent. Jesus told us that if we know how to be good fathers, then how much better a Father is God himself? To see you, as his child, using the gifts he has given and enjoying the way you were created brings a lot of joy to the heart of God. One of the reasons God gave us the gifts in the first place was so he could enjoy sharing them with us. Our gifts are given to be part of the conversation between us and God. The gifts are moments to deepen the relationship between Father and child.

But how do you find this gift of "yes"? Ironically, I have discovered that a lot of people don't want to know their "yes." You may think it is strange that people would not be eager to hear God's description of their destiny. But it's true. Not everyone who is sick wants to get well. Jesus encountered people like this in his ministry. In the gospel of John, Jesus asked a lame man if he wanted to get well. Strangely, the man didn't say, "Yes, I do." Instead, he began to explain why he couldn't be healed.[16] A lot of people are like that man. Instead of receiving the "yes" of Christ, they want to list all the reasons they can't get around to it right now. Jesus never forces it. He reveals himself and offers his "yes." If the person responds, the "yes" is given, and a wonderful adventure begins. If the "yes" is refused, Jesus simply moves on.

If you think about it, you can understand why some people would refuse Jesus's offer of free blessing. Receiving the free gift of Christ changes things. We sense that if we accept this gift, we will have to live differently. We'll have to let go of some things and open our hearts to others. There are no excuses. There is no backing out. Just the gloriously painful process of being made new.

Jesus said he is the Vine and we are the branches.[17] He also said his Father prunes the branches, meaning you and me. And being pruned hurts. The healing that Jesus brings to us forces us to face all the junk in our lives, and some of that junk is hard to deal with. For some it is too painful, and they walk away. For others the way of following Jesus is too demanding, so they also walk away. A lot of people find Jesus very interesting, but few want to crown him Lord of their lives.

So, knowing that a new life will bring changes—including some that are uncomfortable and even painful—do you want your "yes"? I ask this because I believe Jesus is serious about his Kingdom, and only those who are serious about finding the Kingdom will find their "yes." If you really want to accept Jesus's offer, you will let go of everything else to have it. You will have to release your wants and dreams, your ego and treasures; everything in your life that stands between you and Christ has to go. It's the only way the "yes" of Jesus will fit.

Steve Jobs, the late CEO of Apple, said in his commencement address to the 2005 graduating class of Stanford University:

Your time is limited, so don't waste it living someone else's life. Don't be trapped by dogma—which is living with the results of other people's thinking. Don't let the noise of others' opinions drown out your own inner voice. And most important, have the courage to follow your heart and intuition. They somehow already know what you truly want to become. Everything else is secondary.[18]

Jobs was right. Each of us has an identity and destiny unique to us. Being created in the image of God means that each of us bears that divine resemblance in a unique way. The glory of the Creator is revealed in the wonder and divine diversity of his creation. His attributes are infinite, so he never has to repeat himself. Your "yes" is unique to you and is not repeated in the life of anyone else.

The more fully you know your "yes," the more you will understand and appreciate the uniqueness of who you are. Knowing that your "yes" was given only to you will free you to pursue your destiny without concern for how it might compare to anyone else's calling. You are the *only* one who can pursue the unique "yes" that God gave to you.

The "Yes" of You

*Only God can tell you
who you really are*

> I will also give him a white stone, and on the stone a new
> name is inscribed that no one knows except the one who
> receives it.
>
> —JESUS (REVELATION 2:17, HCSB)

His name is Coach. Well, not actually. His real name is Les Steckel,
but everyone, including his wife, calls him Coach. I got to know
Coach when he was hired as the offensive coordinator of the Tennessee
Titans, the NFL franchise in Nashville, and he, his wife, Chris, and their
three children became members of Brentwood Baptist Church. Hanging
around Coach, I observed a side of professional sports most people don't
get to see. Now I have new respect for the sacrifices the coaches, players,
and families have to make to be competitive at that level. Because of my
friendship with Les, I began to follow the Titans and stayed with the
team right until the Super Bowl loss when Kevin Dyson was tackled one
yard short of a game-tying touchdown. We're still trying to get over that
one.[1]

Knowing Les allowed me to see that sometimes life doesn't work
out the way it should, even for good guys like him. Not long after the
Super Bowl season, Les left the Titans for a position with the Tampa Bay

Buccaneers. There was a lot of speculation in the local media about why Les had taken the new job, and none of it was even close to the truth. Regardless, fans of the Titans became frustrated with Les. (As I said, being with Les allowed me to see a side of professional sports most people don't see.)

Les kept his residence in Brentwood, near our church, and moved to Tampa to start his new job. After a season in which the Buccaneers broke most of their offensive records, Les was fired by Tampa Bay. Talk about irony. And, again, most of what the media reported was inaccurate. Les and Chris moved back home to Nashville.

He had time to figure out his next step since he had two years left on his contract. Then two amazing things happened. First, Les became a volunteer coach for his son Luke's football team. With an NFL offensive coordinator on the sideline, the Brentwood High Bruins won the state championship that year. And Luke made the game-saving interception! (I am not making this up.) Second, Les began to lead a men's Tuesday-morning Bible study.

Of all the things our church has ever done for men, this weekly Bible study had one of the greatest impacts. Les would begin each session by reviewing the NFL games from the previous weekend, especially any significant plays during the Monday-night game. He would run a tape of the play and then break it down for the men. He would talk about every player and what each was responsible for. And then, without missing a beat, he would turn the points he was making about football into life lessons for the men in the Bible study. Les would drive the points home with Scripture.

Once, he talked about how to run a two-minute drill. When the team is behind and time is running out, teams use specific plays and different ways of running them so time doesn't expire before they have a good chance to score. To make his point, he turned to the men and made a signal to huddle up (done by cupping the hands slightly and interlacing the fingers). When the clock is stopped, he said, huddle your team, and make sure everyone knows the next play. At this point he stopped and turned directly to the men. "Now when you huddle with your family..."

He let the image hang in the air. "You don't huddle with your family?" he asked in mock surprise. "Well, there's your problem. Your kids are split out wide, and your wife can't get the call. Your family doesn't know the call! Huddle up!"

Every one of the men got his message. What none of us could have foreseen was that God had another assignment for Coach. One day he pulled me aside and said the Fellowship of Christian Athletes had contacted him about becoming their new CEO. What did I think? "Coach, look at your life," I said. "You have spent your entire life coaching. Recently you got to spend a year working with high school coaches and teaching men at our church. FCA looks like the next natural step."

Les took the job, and he has been serving with great success. I've heard the staff of FCA calls him Coach, by the way.

Before someone objects and says we shouldn't refer to people by what they do, let me explain that calling Les "Coach" is an honorary title. He has earned it by being such a vital part of other people's lives. He makes people better. He coaches them, and they acknowledge this by calling him Coach.

More than that, Les's name is Coach. Whether he is on the sideline during an NFL game, or serving as CEO of FCA, or coaching a high school team's offense, or having coffee with a man who has asked for a little counsel, his name is Coach. And because Les knows who he is, he is able to work in any and every circumstance. His identity, solidified in his relationship with Christ, liberates him from the limitations any situation might try to impose on him. Les knows who he is, and because of that, he can do what he does.

But first things first. Let me ask you: Do you know who you are? Do you know your name? Don't look on your driver's license, because you won't find your real name there. The identity I'm talking about is written deep in your soul and can be found only by looking there. Why? Because that's where God put it. Your identity is revealed in a deep encounter with Christ.

FINDING OUR IDENTITIES

Researchers tell us that newborns spend most of their time searching their environment and discovering what is "me" and "not me." A baby begins to understand that the bed she lies in is "not me." Mom and Dad are "not me." But the wiggly things on the end of her arm are "me." So are the feet at the end of her legs and the body in between.

In reality, this process of discovery never stops. We go through life checking our environment and finding out what is and is not "me." Your dad might want you to excel in sports, but is that you? Your pastor might suggest that you would benefit from going to seminary, but is that you? Your friends might tell you to run for homecoming queen or class president or be in charge of decorations for the prom. Are any of these you?

Our culture pressures us to conform to a predetermined norm. Like Goldilocks in the house of the three bears, we mix and match expectations and norms, discarding everything that we think is "not me" until we find what we think is just right. The problem with that approach is that it's a negative process. We find what is "me" by default. We eliminate all the stuff that seems not to be "me" and see what is left. Now it gets confusing, because what is left is a crazy quilt of mixed expectations, desires, passions, and behaviors that still tends to blur the picture. Instead of being a portrait of what is truly "me," it is a catchall of the things that are less "not me" than all the stuff that got discarded.

What if we could begin the process another way? What if we started out with a firm understanding of me before we encountered the influences and expectations of the rest of the world? What if the first statement was "This is me," and we measured every other influence and expectation against that starting point? Think how freeing that would be. Instead of deciding who I am through the trial-and-error process discussed earlier, I could just eliminate all the influences that don't match who I am. I could be proactive about living in the world based on my true identity, not hunting around, hoping to assemble an identity out of the influences and pressures I encounter in life.

You might be thinking that would be great, but once you have lived on this earth for a number of years, you are already a product of the combined influences and expectations you have been exposed to. You can't go back and start all over again.

Why not?

One image that is often used to describe Christian conversion is a transformation of bad to good or dark to light. Those metaphors still hold true, but there is another way to understand conversion that might be more helpful. What if conversion is the realization that the Spirit of God covers us in our real essence? What if we now understand that most of what we have been told about ourselves is a lie? What if Christ's top priority is not to convince us that we are abject failures but to reveal how beautiful we are in him? What if his first work in us is to restore to its original luster the image of God in which we were created? What if we are not orphans in the universe but children of God, heirs to the promise Christ lived in front of us?

In other words, what if the message of the gospel and the effect of conversion are to restore hope in us rather than to impress us with how terrible our fallen condition is? (Don't we know already that we're sinners, separated from God and in desperate need of a Savior?) If Jesus is not as interested in hammering us about our sin as in restoring us to the people God created us to be, would we act differently? live differently? be different toward others? Would we find in this truth a way to change, to live differently, to become a new person?

My answer is yes, and I'm not alone.

Henri Nouwen was challenged by a young agnostic friend to write about his faith in Christ—but to write for the ordinary person on the street. Nouwen at first tried to get out of doing what his friend had requested. He knew it would be extremely difficult. But then he relented and ended up writing a short but profound book, *Life of the Beloved.*

Nouwen began writing with these words: "Ever since you asked me to write for you and your friends about the spiritual life, I have been wondering if there might be one word I would want most of you to remember when you finished reading all I wish to say...it is the word 'Beloved.'"[2] One of the most respected and insightful writers on the subject of Christian spirituality struggled to define the Christian faith and then stumbled upon one word, *beloved.* The essence of the gospel is this: we are the objects of God's relentless love. The "yes" of God is spoken in the love of God, which we don't deserve and can't earn. We are loved, not because we are worthy of love, but because God is, in his essence, *love.*[3]

Brennan Manning picks up this same theme in his book *The Ragamuffin Gospel:* "Never confuse your perception of yourself with the mystery that you really are accepted."[4] This is where an accurate, unimpeachable self-awareness begins. Not with what we look like or what we have or have not accomplished. It has nothing to do with how talented we are or whether we make friends easily. The gospel, the foundational truth of our existence, is that we are *loved by God.* Everything else flows from that eternal reality.

We don't go from being adults to infants in the cradle, but the change is so profound, so fundamentally transformative to our basic natures, that we become, in essence, born again. One of the aspects of this experience is realizing that because Christ loves you, you are a child of the Kingdom. This is fundamentally a new identity for each of us. We now understand that no matter what anyone else says, we are known and loved, chosen and cherished. The identifying sentences of our lives change. We no longer say, "I am a victim," "I am broken," "I am lost," or "I am abandoned." Now we say, "I am his."

And because so many of us don't understand this truth about our identity, we end up conflicted and confused about who we really are and how we should live. Eric Clapton, the legendary guitarist, tells of such a moment in his life. Trying to get healthy after a lifetime of addiction, Clapton had a conversation with a counselor.

> Chris's first question to me, at our very first session, was, "Tell me who you are," a very simple question you would think, but I felt the blood rush up to my face and wanted to yell at her, "How dare you! Don't you know who I am?" Of course, I had no idea who I was, and I was ashamed to admit it.[5]

How can you accomplish anything in your life if the most important existential question of all—"Who am I?"—remains unanswered? When you are constantly searching for your identity, you get lost in a costly trial-and-error search. You try this and try that, changing your direction when the pain is too great to bear. No experience or encounter, no outside influence can tell you who you are. Only Christ can do that.

In Revelation, Jesus promises to give the church in Pergamum a new name: "I will also give that person a white stone with a new name written on it, known only to the one who receives it."[6] This name, given to us by Christ, announces several important realities that determine our new life in him. First, our relationship with God is confirmed. Only he and only we know our names. Second, it confirms our value to him. The name we receive is protected.

Belonging to Christ answers a fundamental question for us: the question of self-worth. For some, having high self-esteem has become a central life goal. Parents feel pressured to supply their children with high self-esteem. The problem, however, is when a person's self-esteem is based on hype, not reality. Too often we lie to our children by telling them they can be anything they want to be—ballerina dancers, firefighters, professional athletes, musicians, scientists. And in America we say anybody can grow up to be president. All you have to do is want your dream badly enough to work for it and never give up. If you can conceive it, you can achieve it.

No you can't.

Let's admit the truth: reality bites. Believing you can be whatever you can imagine, even when you believe with all your heart, won't make it true.

I love basketball. A few years ago a major athletic-shoe company said if I bought their $250 basketball shoes, I could "Be Like Mike," meaning Michael Jordan. At the time I was a forty-something, slightly overweight, married father of two. I could buy the shoes, but I would never be like Mike. I would be the fat white guy standing in the middle of the court in a good-looking pair of shoes. Gravity and lack of talent would make sure I would never be confused with Michael Jordan.

Put yourself in the place of a child who is convinced he can grow up to be a world-class athlete, famous surgeon, or president. If he fails to fulfill his dreams, it's likely he'll believe that he just wasn't dedicated enough. The truth, however, is that he likely is short on talent, savvy, resources, or other necessities.

In her book *Bright-Sided,* Barbara Ehrenreich says we no longer suffer any excuse for failure in our culture.[7] Our culture despises limits of any kind, even when its insistence on denying limits is a bald-faced lie. You can be more committed to a dream than any other human in history has ever been, but that doesn't guarantee you'll succeed. This truth is harsh but necessary.

As Ehrenreich and others have noted, this insistence on the positive has had unexpected consequences. For one thing, as children grow up and encounter situations where they fall far short of first place, some have a difficult time dealing with failure. Colleges have developed workshops for parents of Gen Y students and have coined the phrase *helicopter parents.* Helicopter parents hover over their children and drop down into their children's lives whenever there is a sign of trouble. The parents solve the child's problems, and as a result the child never develops the confidence to solve problems on her own. The child also has trouble learning to trust the reality around her. If she is constantly told that things are not the way they appear, the child learns not to trust what she is seeing. This happens when a child is told "You can be anything" but her experience again and again shouts just the opposite: "You don't have what it takes to be the best!"

Whom will the child believe? Mom and Dad or some naysayer in the school of hard knocks?

The Christian teaching is that people are extremely valuable indeed. But our value is not based on the promise of exceptional achievement or a positive feeling about ourselves. It is grounded in the reality of who God is and what he has done for us in Christ. Christianity calls us to face reality at every level. When Christ called Paul to preach in Rome right under the nose of the Roman emperor, it was not a call to false assurances or illusion. Paul understood that he would one day die for the faith he was preaching.[8]

Jesus worked miracles, and our faith is grounded in the biggest possible miracle: the resurrection of Christ. This is reality, not myth. Of all the world religions, Christianity demands we face the truth in all matters. In a famous parable Jesus told about two men who built houses, one on sand and the other on a rock. When the storms came, the house on the rock stood, but the house built on sand collapsed.[9] Jesus, of course, was helping us see that any life not built on the truth of his teaching won't withstand the storms of life.

As we seek to know who we are, we need to go to the Truth, which is Jesus. He is the only sure foundation upon which to build our lives. We are called to be the children of Truth and to seek truth in every aspect of life. Following Christ means we remove all that is false from our teachings, our business dealings, and our families and relationships.

This removal process extends to having a truthful understanding of our self-worth. If our lives are going to stand the tests, we have to have a self-worth grounded in something more solid than the praise of our parents, teachers, and coaches. Our value isn't found in ourselves but in the unchanging God who created us.

Imago Dei

We are valuable and treasured for no other reason than God says we are. He chose to add us to his creation as the only beings who would bear his image, the *imago Dei*. The Bible introduces humanity into the creation story by way of a conversation that took place among the Persons of the Godhead. "Let us make mankind," God says, "in our image."[10]

Being created in the image of God, reflecting the imago Dei, is the single most important part of the creation story. Like a great piece of art by a famous painter, the work—in this case, us—is valued not because of the work itself but because of the greatness of the Artist. The reason murder is wrong is because taking a human life damages the image of God within the person. While it may be argued that other parts of creation bear traces of God's handiwork, only humanity bears the image of God.

There is considerable debate as to what the image of God actually is and how it impacts our day-to-day lives. Moses was a poet and thus painted his descriptions using large strokes that invited conversation and engagement. While no one is exactly sure, some say the image of God is the soul of the human, but then we argue about what the soul is. Some point out that humans have God's creative abilities, that we can change our environment and create new opportunities and futures. Others say it is the ability to use language, and still others say it is the capacity to be in relationship with God. There has to be something in us that connects to and recognizes a likeness when we encounter God. I recognize God as wholly other, but there has to be something in us, some moment of familiarity that creates a desire for and ultimately makes possible a relationship with God.

The Price

Certainly this is one of the truths of the Incarnation. God graciously chose to meet us largely on our terms, meaning in ways we would recognize. The signature of the Artist gives a painting its value. So with us, the traces of the Master's fingers across our souls remind us that his touch—the touch of his essence left in us—is enough to mark us as priceless.

The true value of an object is often found in the offered payment, not in the demanded price. You can list your home at whatever price you desire, but you will only know its true value when someone makes a firm offer. When you apply this standard to humanity, and to you and me individually, you find that we are beyond priceless. On the day when the price for our lives was demanded, God gave up the best he had, the life of his only Son, to secure our salvation.

In those lonely hours in Gethsemane, with his disciples sleeping nearby and soldiers coming quickly behind Judas to arrest him, Jesus looked into the cup of the demands of justice and asked God if the cup could be taken away. But the mercy of God held the cup steady. Justice would be satisfied in the hours that followed. Sin would exact its full cost, and Jesus would pay it all. The imago Dei, damaged in the Fall almost to the point of being unrecognizable, would be restored by the abiding presence of Christ's Spirit in our lives. We are created in the image of God and bought with the life of the Son. That's how much we are worth.

Living from the Center

When you accept the full value that God places on your life, there is integrity in your living. It means that who you are, what you do, and how you live all line up. There is an honesty in answering the "Who am I?" question the same way in every aspect of your life. You don't try to make a bigger deal about your accomplishments when you are talking to someone who might be able to help you get ahead rather than the summer intern or a member of the cleaning crew. Instead, you are more than happy to be who God made you to be and are thankful for the value he places on you.

Knowing who you are, you begin to live from the center of your essence. Your identity is lived out and revealed in all aspects of your life. Your choices are not made on the outside and then pulled into your life. Now your choices begin on the inside, where you know who you are in Christ. You then choose what is best, meaning in line with who God says you are.

That means sometimes you will say no to things that are important and good but are not good or best for you. This is what Paul told Christians in the first century when he wrote, "All things are permissible for me, but not all things are beneficial for me."[11] Can you take on a volunteer position as chair of your town's annual fund drive to supply books for the school or town library? Perhaps. But "Should I do it?" is quite another question.

LIVING TRUE TO YOU

Jeannie and I are the proud parents of twin sons, Chris and Craig. Boys are always a challenge to raise well. Two boys are, well, twice the challenge. Both Chris and Craig, in their own ways, were always testing their strength by pushing back against any limits we imposed on them. As you can imagine, we ended up having long conversations about behavior. In those moments here is what we found out. The best way to discipline our sons was not with threats but with reminders of who they really are. A typical conversation would go like this.

Jeannie and I would remind them that we have known them since before they were born. We have sonogram pictures of both sons together before they were born, and we can tell you which boy is which from those pictures. We would tell our sons, "We have always known you to be this kind of young man," and we would list concrete incidents when they had been their best and most authentic selves. Our sons would each recognize themselves in the telling.

Then we would talk about the behavior in question and say, "This recent behavior doesn't line up with the person we know you to be. Why didn't you trust yourself enough, why didn't you believe in yourself enough in this situation to be who you really are?"

More times than not, this would lead to a lengthy discussion of who they are as individuals and the type of men they were aspiring to become. We would help them see why the behavior in question was not going to help them achieve their goals to become their best selves in Christ. As a result, Chris and Craig would walk away understanding who they are at just a little deeper level.

Do you see the parallel with what our Father is trying to teach us, using the identity he has given us as the measure of what we should and can become? What difference would it make if we deeply understood who we are in Christ and were free to live out that identity without fear? What if we found the courage to live from the inside out, from our true selves anchored in our relationship with Christ?

LET YOUR "YES" BE "YES"

"Let your yes be yes and your no be no," Jesus taught.[12] We always put the emphasis on the "yes" and the "no" in that teaching. What would happen if we put the emphasis on "your"? Let *your* "yes" be "yes." Let *your* "no" be "no." It would relieve us of so much pressure if we knew who we were and then were free to say "yes" and "no" based on an accurate understanding of that identity.

Understand that the "yes" God gives you demands that you live in a different way. If you know what you are worth, you will no longer live in a way that devalues who you are. You will not give in to things that cheapen what God has paid the highest price to save.

You have to push away a lot of superficial stuff to get to the essence of your identity. You find out the most important things about yourself, including your identity, in quiet moments. You can't be connected and available 24/7 if you really want to know who you are. Our world seems determined never to give us a moment of solitude. So you have to push back against the growing wave of noise and digital data. It's in solitude that you can ask the hard questions about who you are and discover the distinctive alchemy of genetics, experience, education, and nurture that makes you uniquely you. As you take this journey, guided by the One who created you, you will know you are fearfully and wonderfully and uniquely made.

The "Yes" of Destiny

What your true identity says about why you're here

> "For I know the plans I have for you," declares the LORD,
> "plans to prosper you and not to harm you, plans to give
> you hope and a future."
>
> —JEREMIAH 29:11

I enjoy sports. If it's on television and if someone is trying to beat somebody else, I'm going to watch it. There have been moments in some games I will never forget. Michael Jordan and the Chicago Bulls against the Cleveland Cavs in the 1989 NBA playoffs with time running out and everyone in the arena knowing Jordan was going to take the last shot. Jordan pulled up in front of Craig Ehlo and *boom*...won the game with a last-second jumper! He did the same thing in 1998 against the Utah Jazz. Okay, there was a little push on Bryon Russell, but Jordan made the shot.

It was a great player in a great moment—destiny! John Elway huddled his Denver Broncos against the Cleveland Browns in the 1986 AFC Championship game. Time was running out, and Denver had to go the length of the field to score and win the game. They did, and from that moment on, every football fan would talk about John Elway and "The Drive." Great player, great moment, destiny!

Destiny applies to much more of life than athletic contests, however.

In 1940, with the Nazi threat rising in Europe, a struggling politician became prime minister of Great Britain. With German U-boats off the coast of England and Nazi bombers overhead, Winston Churchill led the British people through what has been known ever since as their "finest hour." Churchill had met his destiny.

Fans of history know much about destiny, the moment when events move to a point of crisis and the major players rise to the challenge. It's the volatile, unpredictable intersection of danger and opportunity when a man or woman with vision and particular gifts makes a courageous stand. The moment is rarely as dramatic as Winston Churchill rallying the British people to battle the daunting military force of Nazi Germany, but someone or something will be threatened, and at that moment a person will meet his destiny. Maybe this person's actions won't seem all that important at the moment. It could be nothing more than a tired African American woman riding home from work on a city bus and refusing to give up her seat and move to the back. Rosa Parks silently declared her full humanity while using public transportation in Montgomery, Alabama, and things started to change. A candle, however small, will push back the darkness just a little bit. Perhaps no one will ever know this side of eternity about the sacrifice that was made to keep one last candle from going out.

In the winter of 1944, the Germans surprised the Allies with a major offensive that became the Battle of the Bulge. Weather kept the Allies from mounting an aggressive counterattack in the brutal cold. But countless small units of soldiers in forgotten villages made their stand. They would delay the German units for one hour, sometimes for a day, and eventually the Battle of the Bulge was won. The war in the European theater was won, not in the massive Allied response that followed this battle, but in unknown skirmishes where ragtag Allied units made German units suffer casualties and delays. The outcome of the war hung in the balance, and these soldiers held their ground and changed everything.

That's destiny.

THE IMPORTANCE OF "WHY"

When Christians talk about destiny, we are not referring to the inevitable conclusion of a hero's story as decreed by the gods. That is the fabled destiny of ancient mythology, but it has nothing to do with God's work on earth, using people to carry out his purposes. Destiny is not a fixed outcome for your life. There is no act of fate at work. Instead, I use the term to describe the invitation you and I have as believers to be involved in the redemptive work of Christ in his world. We have been asked to join God's work of reconciling the world.

That alone causes us to stop and be silent when we soberly consider the magnitude of our calling. But it is even bigger than that. Not only are we allied with God in the work of his Kingdom on earth, but we are enlisted in this work after first being cast out of our original home. We were exiled from the garden along with Adam and Eve. Now we have been restored to fellowship with him. We have been reconciled to the Father we had rejected. And we join him in reconciling all creation to its original relationship with its Creator.

In the early part of Genesis, God condemned humanity to work without reward.

> To Adam he said, "Because you listened to your wife and ate
> fruit from the tree about which I commanded you, 'You must
> not eat from it,'
>
> "Cursed is the ground because of you;
>> through painful toil you will eat food from it
>> all the days of your life.
> It will produce thorns and thistles for you,
>> and you will eat the plants of the field.
> By the sweat of your brow
>> you will eat your food

until you return to the ground,
>   since from it you were taken;
> for dust you are
>   and to dust you will return."[1]

None of us would want to hear these words from God. Adam knew that from that moment on, he would work, sweat, and worry. We know the truth of this because we experience it nearly every day. We work, but what does it matter? Is the world any better because we showed up on time? If it is, the improvement is short lived. Life, sooner or later, drains us. It seems to rob us of meaning. In short, we have lost the "why" of life.

One of the things we lost in Genesis 3 was meaning. We go to work five days a week, year after year, and nothing seems to improve for long. At the end of the day, we return home with the empty feeling of knowing we have to repeat the entire process all over again in just a few hours. Like Sisyphus, we roll the stone up the hill only to find the stone rolled back down to the bottom while we were sleeping.

Viktor Frankl was an Austrian psychiatrist who survived the concentration camps of Nazi Germany. While a prisoner, Frankl began to notice something about his fellow prisoners. There was a marked difference between those who survived and those who didn't. Survivors, according to Frankl, were able to find meaning in their suffering. They endured the pain in order to get to something or someone important, perhaps to see their children again or to return to working on an important project. Frankl's motivation was to rewrite the manuscript of his book that was destroyed when he was arrested.

From this experience Frankl concluded that meaning, not pleasure or power, is the most basic human need.[2] He wrote that if people can understand their "why," they will be able to endure almost anything.[3] If you know why you are going through something, no matter how painful the trial, you have a much better chance of getting through it. The reverse is also true. Without knowing the why, you won't be able to endure. You need a reason to stand up against whatever life throws at you.

One of the reasons life is so difficult is that much of it makes no apparent sense. We suffer, but it serves no apparent purpose. An innocent motorist is killed when a drunk driver runs a red light. This makes no sense. If there were justice, the guilty driver would die, but that often is not the outcome. The family and friends who lost a person they love are left to wonder why. The absence of a reasonable why can affect any area of our lives, from the loss of a friendship, the loss of a job, a chronic illness, the constant news of atrocities committed in some war where neither side seems good or right.

At times when we suffer, we suspect it's a result of something we did in the past, perhaps even something unintentional. And at times we suffer the consequences for what others did—things we had absolutely no control over. We are innocent bystanders of crime, gossip, greed, self-centeredness, lies, or a lack of generosity and compassion. People seem to be determined to make life unnecessarily hard for the rest of us. You can try to make sense of these things, but you'll be frustrated. The most brilliant theologians and philosophers have tried, and I still have never read a logical, convincing explanation for the problem of injustice, evil against innocent persons, and the suffering we all share.

One thought haunts me every time I drive past a cemetery: we will live, love, work, and then die. And then what? What will remain of our hard work, our investment of talents and skills, and our repeated attempts to make the world a better place? This universal frustration is one of the arguments used to prove the afterlife. If God is going to make things right, he is going to need a time and place to do that, which means there has to be another time and place beyond this world. Because things certainly aren't right in the here and now.

The curse of Adam means that life will not be a constant experience of peace and fulfillment. But neither did God put us on earth to endure continual confusion and frustration. And here is a big part of the good news of Jesus: he gives us our "why." Christ came to us, offering life and meaning. He has invited us to follow him and in doing so to find our purpose within his purpose. Jesus knew his why, and his why now becomes our why.

If that is true, we need to learn about the why of Jesus. A good place to start is with an incident that took place in Jesus's hometown.

THE "YES" OF JESUS

Jesus returned to his home village of Nazareth. Stories of his ministry had spread back to the people who had known him when he was growing up. On the Sabbath, Jesus was asked to read from the scroll of Isaiah.

Unrolling it, he found the place where it is written:

"The Spirit of the Lord is on me,
    because he has anointed me
    to proclaim good news to the poor.
He has sent me to proclaim freedom for the prisoners
    and recovery of sight for the blind,
to set the oppressed free,
    to proclaim the year of the Lord's favor."

Then he rolled up the scroll, gave it back to the attendant
and sat down. The eyes of everyone in the synagogue were
fastened on him. He began by saying to them, "Today this
scripture is fulfilled in your hearing."[4]

Experts in work productivity often help a client by first having her write a personal mission statement. Jesus seems to have pointed to the passage in Isaiah 61 as his mission statement. He understood his life as being the fulfillment of the prophet's words. These verses were Jesus's "yes," his destiny. He would filter every moment, every decision through these verses. The words of Isaiah acted as a sort of lens that focused the energy and passion of Jesus's life and work. He would not allow his ministry to become cluttered or diffused by the expectations of others. He would not allow opposition, no matter how powerful, to distract him from his purposes.

We should not be surprised to know that our destiny flows out of his. In defending his apostleship, Paul described his ministry as flowing from the ministry of Christ: "If anyone is in Christ, the new creation has come: The old has gone, the new is here! All this is from God, who reconciled us to himself through Christ and gave us the ministry of reconciliation."[5]

Paul saw his ministry of reconciliation as being an extension of the reconciliation ministry of Jesus. This is part of our restoration. What we lost in the Fall we regained in the resurrection of Jesus. As Christ-followers, we are called to join Christ in his work by taking our gifts and resources to the broken places in and around our communities. We are called to the ministry of reconciling people to God.

THE POWER TO NAME

One of the greatest powers God gave us is the power to name. Identifying something is the first step in controlling it. Doctors diagnose, or name, a disease and then prescribe an effective treatment. A counselor will work with a struggling couple to carefully define the problem, because until the problem is named, the couple can't move forward in healing their marriage. Scientists precisely write the presenting question of their experiments, because only an accurate statement of the problem can lead to a successful conclusion. The same is true in our lives. Jesus invites us to define the meaning of our lives, which leads to the pursuit of our destiny.

Viktor Frankl noted that we should not ask what the meaning of life is but understand we are asked to give a meaning to our lives.[6] Jesus named his meaning as he read Isaiah 61 in Nazareth. By extension, we name our meaning as we align our lives with the ultimate destiny of Christ. We echo back to Christ the gracious "yes" he has spoken to us. Our destiny is to be present with Christ in the moments when his "yes" can be spoken through us.

COURAGE IN THE MOMENT

Destiny is not determined by whether a heroine is remembered in history for her valiant acts. Rather, a heroine fulfills her destiny when she is faithful and brave in the face of danger.

Charles Strobel is a well-known Catholic priest in Nashville. He is an advocate for the homeless and the founder of Nashville's Room In The Inn. During the winter months Strobel engages churches to join the effort to provide overnight housing for the homeless. Countless lives, of those served and of those serving, have been affected because of his ministry. Has he eradicated homelessness? Of course not. But he has been brave and courageous in the fight.

Nashville's homeless have no better advocate than Charles Strobel. It began with a moment of great need: homeless people were cold. That need was met with the intense passion of a priest who, in the lives of the homeless, saw Christ sleeping outside and then did something about it. That's destiny.

Earlier we mentioned Dr. Ben Carson. His story of overcoming poverty will deeply move any reader. He was raised by a single mother in Detroit. Sonya Carson, Ben's mother, was determined that her two sons, Ben and Curtis, were not going to become victims of the inner-city struggles that have claimed so many young lives. She limited their television time, made them check out books from the library, and demanded they succeed in school. Ben did not start out well, but his mother determined he could do better. When he did do better, she still wasn't satisfied.

"All right, Bennie, you've started improving," his mother said, "and you're going to keep on improving."[7] And he did, right on through high school, college, and medical school until he had become one of the nation's preeminent pediatric neurosurgeons. There was a great challenge: how does a single mom raise two boys in inner-city Detroit? There was a great woman, Sonya Carson, who found a way. A great challenge met by great courage. That's destiny.

NAMING THE REASON

Most of us never think about our lives in terms of our destiny. We simply get up and do the next thing we know to do. In the distant past, we may have had some late-night bull sessions with our teenage friends, dreaming about what we would do when we grew up. But then life happened. We graduated and got jobs. We had responsibilities to shoulder and deadlines to meet. Whatever dreams we had about making a difference in the world got filed away under "someday."

We didn't intend for it to happen that way, and we still plan to get back to our dreams one day. But right now there simply is no time. We keep postponing our destiny until "no time" becomes "no chance," and something in us dies. Our dreams were slowly suffocated under the numbing weight of obligations and expectations.

Don't settle for a numb life. Don't accept that everyday life is more powerful than God's calling in your life. The dream is the reason you were born. Frederick Buechner wrote, "The place God calls you is the place where your deep gladness and the world's deep hunger meet."[8] Our destiny begins with deep gladness, with the dreams of how our talents can be used to restore creation and all who are part of creation back to God's original dream. In Matthew 25, Jesus celebrated the ministry of encountering need and brokenness.

Then the King will say to those on his right, "Come, you who are blessed by my Father; take your inheritance, the kingdom prepared for you since the creation of the world. For I was

hungry and you gave me something to eat, I was thirsty and
you gave me something to drink, I was a stranger and you
invited me in, I needed clothes and you clothed me, I was
sick and you looked after me, I was in prison and you came
to visit me."[9]

Wherever there is a need, wherever there is a part of creation that
does not reflect the glory of the Artist who created it, we are called to restore the original beauty in the power of the Risen Christ. This is the final
glory of redemption:

For the creation waits in eager expectation for the children of
God to be revealed. For the creation was subjected to frustration, not by its own choice, but by the will of the one who
subjected it.[10]

The completion of creation, the fulfillment of all the potential of
God's glorious work in Genesis 1, is now waiting for us to discover our
destiny in Christ. When we fulfill that destiny, we will have joined with
Christ in fulfilling the destiny of all of creation.

DESTINY IS NOT THE SAME AS YOUR JOB

Let's be careful not to confuse calling with career. While we may be
called to a particular destiny in Christ, our careers may or may not be
direct expressions of our callings. In my case, my calling does involve my
career, and I know of other people whose callings are supported by, en-
hanced by, and expanded through their careers. But their careers are not
necessarily their callings. Paul, for instance, was a tentmaker, but his calling was to be an apostle.

I have a friend who is a very successful business leader. He has a deep
love for Christ that shapes every decision of his life. He has told me that

he sometimes thinks he should go into vocational ministry. My counsel to him is that he should stay where he is. Because he is so successful and admired, his business career has given him a platform he could never achieve as a professional minister. The only reason some people seek out his counsel is his reputation in the business community. And when he mentors those he has agreed to work with, he teaches them about integrity and servant leadership in terms of Christ's teaching. They see that what he is saying to them has been lived out and tested in his life. His career gives him a platform to express his destiny in Christ, but his calling is developing Christlike leaders.

C. Michael Thompson writes in his book *The Congruent Life,* "No kind of work is inherently more meaningful than any other; all work is capable of addressing our core needs for meaning and purpose."[11] Your work could be an expression of your destiny, but it doesn't have to be. The meaning your work possesses depends on what meaning you assign to it. Our meaning flows out of our relationship with Christ. He is our ultimate source of meaning and value.[12] As Christ was sent to reconcile the world to God, we also, like Paul, have a ministry of reconciliation. That is, God is working with us and through us to pull the world back into a vital relationship with him. Our careers can support this mission, but our work need not be our mission.

Finding Destiny

You don't find your destiny; your destiny finds you. Your destiny flows out of your identity, the name Christ has placed deep inside you. To find your destiny involves a quiet search of your own depths as well as your relationship with Christ. Parker Palmer wrote, "Vocation does not come from willfulness. It comes from listening."[13] As we spend time in prayer and in the examination of our lives, we will begin to see how Christ has chosen to reveal himself in us and through us.

To make this more practical, begin by asking yourself a couple of simple questions. First, *what are my gifts?* This is a little uncomfortable for most of us. We are taught not to talk too much about ourselves or to say that we are pretty good at something. That sounds too much like the sin of pride. But the fact is, Jesus gave you at least one spiritual gift. For the building up of his body, which is the church, Jesus gave each believer abilities and capabilities to serve the church and the church's mission. Paul told the Christians in Ephesus:

> There is one body and one Spirit, just as you were called to one
> hope when you were called; one Lord, one faith, one baptism;
> one God and Father of all, who is over all and through all and
> in all.
>   But to each one of us grace has been given as Christ
> apportioned it.[14]

Here is an essential truth: Everyone has something to add to the body of Christ, yet no one has all the gifts. We are created and designed so that together we better express the fullness of Christ and his mission of reconciliation.

Here is the second question: *Where is there brokenness around me? Ask yourself, Where is there pain? What part of my world would Jesus touch if he walked my streets?*

If your world is like mine, you won't have to look far. Russell Conwell, a famous Baptist minister and the founder of Temple University, told a story about a Persian farmer who sold his farm to go look for diamonds, only to discover later that a diamond mine had been found in his own backyard.[15] The best place to start looking for your treasure is in your own backyard. Your destiny may not include adventurous journeys around the world. To find your destiny, you might need merely to cross the street. Jesus never traveled far from the places he had known as a child.

God started human civilization in a garden with Adam and Eve. He did not give Adam the whole world but one garden to tend.[16] Adam was responsible for only one area that surrounded where he lived. Likewise, we are called to partner with God in his redemptive work in a focused area. In fact, don't be surprised if the opportunity seems a little small. That's fine. God will allow you to start small, teach you valuable lessons as you obey his leading, and allow you to grow from there. As you see God use your gifts, your faithful confidence in his work will allow God to use you in ever-expanding opportunities. But don't let your frustrations, doubts, and questioning get out of hand. We aren't responsible for everything, just the moment to which we are called.

And as you pursue your destiny in Christ, don't be surprised if failure is part of the journey. Trial and error generally accompany this process. If you find something doesn't work, don't be afraid to say it's not working, and go find something else. You can make only two mistakes here. The first is pushing yourself into a situation that doesn't match your gifts or your wiring. Pedaling a broken bicycle won't make you go faster. Sometimes you need to get off and try something else. The other mistake? Quitting. Someone somewhere is broken, lost, and confused, and you are destined to be available when he needs help the most. Make sure you meet that moment.

DESTINY AS WORSHIP

When I was growing up in Alabama, Mr. Green was the janitor at our little church. I cannot fully describe how clean our church was. The floors were waxed to the point where they were almost too slick to walk on. The carpets were vacuumed, and the chairs were dusted. When you would talk to Mr. Green, he would say, "Jesus will be here on Sunday." For me, Mr. Green was the living example of Paul's teaching to the Christians in Colossae: "Do it all in the name of the Lord Jesus."[17] Mr. Green had turned the drudgery of cleaning a building into an act of worship. He had made his work an offering to Christ. There was a need, and he had given this need great meaning. He was cleaning the church for Jesus. He fulfilled his destiny.

If Mr. Green's life and work were not significant, why am I still talking about it forty years later? Why is his name included in this book? That's destiny.

Judy Campbell loves to garden. She turned her sizable backyard into a botanical garden that would rival most public gardens with its walking paths, benches, small ponds, and lots of blooming flowers. "It's the place where Jesus and I work together," she told me as she gave me a tour one afternoon. "You know, the first place God made was a garden." She prays for friends when she works in the garden. In a city bustling with frantic sounds, she has created an oasis. She has reclaimed her little section of creation—redeemed it—for its intended purpose.

That garden is a place where God and his children meet. Friends come by and sit in the garden. Sometimes they talk with this marvelous gardener but most of the time not. People come to pray. They come to rest. They come to remember. They find Jesus there just as she does. This is her destiny.

You want a short definition for destiny? How's this: destiny is the moment God uses the "yes" in you to ignite his "yes" in another person. Probably no one said it better than Saint Francis. He was familiar with destiny.

Lord, make me an instrument of your peace.
Where there is hatred, let me sow love;
where there is injury, pardon;
where there is doubt, faith;
where there is despair, hope;
where there is darkness, light;
and where there is sadness, joy.
O Divine Master, grant that I may not so much seek

to be consoled as to console;
to be understood as to understand;
to be loved as to love.
For it is in giving that we receive;
it is in pardoning that we are pardoned;
and it is in dying that we are born to eternal life.
Amen.[18]

The "Yes" of Authentic Relationships

*You need other people to
help you follow your "yes"*

This is how we know what love is: Jesus Christ laid down
his life for us. And we ought to lay down our lives for our
brothers and sisters.

—1 John 3:16

An excited couple comes into my office, walking close together and holding hands. They sit on the couch, as close as two people can sit and still be occupying two separate spaces. Then they tell me how they met and fell in love. They have set the date and are planning their wedding. Would I, they wonder, officiate? I get out my calendar, and we talk about the date and what they are expecting from me in this process. I find out if they have scheduled their required premarital-counseling sessions and have filled out all the forms for the use of our church sanctuary.

Then I ask the big question: "Why do you want to get married?" For some reason this question catches couples off guard. They are in love. Why would anyone need more reasons than that? But I press for something deeper, and eventually one of them risks an answer.

"I need her," he will say. "She makes me complete."

"Yeah, that's it," the bride-to-be echoes. "It's as if I wasn't a whole person until I met him."

THE *ROCKY* THEORY OF LOVE

This is what I call the *Rocky* Theory of Love. In the movie *Rocky* (yes, I am old enough to have seen *Rocky* when it was first shown in theaters), Paulie asks Rocky what the boxer sees in Paulie's sister, Adrian. "She fills gaps," Rocky says. "She's got gaps. I got gaps. Together we fill gaps."[1] But two wounded people, no matter how much they love each other, do not make a healthy marriage. Two wounded people make a hospital.

Over and over, broken people enter into all kinds of relationships looking for the other party to make them whole. A man assumes his wife will "take care of him." While this expectation is never fully verbalized, for most men the vision of marriage includes a woman who will somehow solve their inner pain. Women get married assuming the marriage relationship will add the missing ingredient to their lives. These assumptions, which have their origins in childhood or adolescence, are that another person will somehow fill a hole in one's heart.

It rarely works out, since the other people are looking for people to fill gaps in their lives as well. Every life has holes in it, and every person wants to have the holes filled. The insistence on getting the need met puts so much pressure on the relationship that it often breaks down.

Everyone wants to be taken care of, but few of us are interested in taking care of someone else. When the pursuit of being "made complete" is carried into marriage, disappointment is sure to follow. The person who seeks wholeness from the other, and eventually realizes that the other person keeps failing to get the job done, becomes bitter and hostile. Meanwhile, the one who is constantly faced with his or her partner's neediness grows tired of being asked to pour more of himself or herself into a leaking person. No matter how committed people are in a relationship, they can't provide the healing their partner needs.

Sadly, the worn-out partner eventually pushes away just to avoid being consumed in a spouse's unending demands. This is seen most tragically in marriages, but it takes place in friendships as well. For most people, friendships have become mechanical and pragmatic, described in terms of how useful the relationship is in helping an individual realize his or her own goals. We connect with people; we network with our friends. A friendship is seen not as a relationship having intrinsic value but as an arrangement that holds the potential for personal benefit.

A "friend" might be able to open doors that would advance a career or present other opportunities. Let's be honest. This is not a friendship; it is a business arrangement—and a one-sided arrangement at that. And if a friend can no longer provide new opportunities for the other, the friendship is dropped. Friendships have become assets and commodities, things to be leveraged for personal benefit and future payoffs. No wonder people prefer to text their friends instead of meeting in person. Something human has been lost from our relationships. Friends have become functions.

RELATIONSHIPS FROM "YES"

But what happens if we approach a relationship not from a sense of need but from a sense of our "yes"? That is, what if we came into a relationship seeking to understand how we could best serve the other person? What if we didn't expect the other to fill gaps or needs in our lives? What if the other was free to be who he or she is, on the same basis that we have been liberated to be who we are in Christ?

A few years ago I was talking to my wife about our relationship and the idea of "needing" each other. Neither of us liked that word. *Need* no longer accurately described our relationship. Fact is, neither one of us needs the other. If one of us were to die, the other would go on living. We would grieve. We would hurt. But we would still live without having the other in our life.

While we decided we didn't need each other, we were happy to admit that we really want each other. We like being together, and things are better when we can share them. There has never been any question about this. We could survive alone, without each other. But we far prefer to go through life together. Maybe this doesn't sound particularly romantic; it might not meet the definition of "smitten soul mates." But being wanted is a lot more fun than being needed.

If I were "needed," I would be responsible for providing something in Jeannie's life. But, ultimately, Jeannie is responsible for her own life, as I am responsible for mine. It's not possible for her to make me happy. She can't give my life meaning. She can only share who she is. She gives me love because she chooses to, not because I demand it.

Love of this type comes out of the overflow of Christ's love in us. Love like this makes no demands. It is given the same way Jesus gives his love to us—freely. I give my love to my wife because I choose to do so. I give it with no demand that she reciprocate. She knows her "yes," and I know mine. Again, this may not sound like soft music and a moonlit stroll, but living out of the "yes" of our own identities means we are free to love the other for the other's sake, without looking for compensation. It's as close to the love described in 1 Corinthians 13 as I have ever come.

In our most reflective moments, we all would confess that relationships—not things—are what make living worthwhile. Objects do not warrant our loyalty, service, or love. So why do we "interface" with each other or "play in" to a conversation? Why do we regard other people as somehow less valuable, less human than we are? I guess it's because things are easier to manage. It's impossible to control other people, because each of us is a free moral agent. But regarding people as objects might give us the illusion that we are in control. Think what the Velveteen Rabbit teaches us.[2] When you are loved, your buttons fall off and your fur gets rubbed thin. Love hurts. And real love really hurts. An inanimate object is much easier to contend with.

But what if we were able to approach the other person, filled with the love of Christ—comfortable in who we are in him and confident of our self-worth because of him? Would that change how we approach other people? Would that free us up to simply love others for who they are and not demand anything from them?

No one can meet my needs but Christ. To ask my wife or anyone else to meet them is to ask people to do what only God can do. If we lived according to this truth, how would it transform our understanding of relationships? Relationships are transformed for the better when we love without expecting anything in return. We don't have to manipulate the other person to get our needs met. We can let them be who they are. We can celebrate with their successes and grieve with their losses without jealousy or possessiveness. Out of the overflow of his own life, Jesus loved the people he encountered. Because he is complete in himself, he can extend himself even when his love isn't returned.

THE TRIANGLE OF "YES"

Matthew and Mark tell the story of a lawyer who asked Jesus a question: "Teacher, which is the greatest commandment?"[3] He asked the question to trick Jesus. All the leading rabbis had their favorite verses, and it was somewhat of a parlor game to argue about the greatest law. Jesus ran the risk of alienating some of his listeners by siding with one teacher over another. So it's interesting how he chose to answer.

Mark records that Jesus first quoted the Shema: "Hear, O Israel: The Lord our God, the Lord is one. Love the Lord your God with all your heart and with all your soul and with all your mind and with all your strength."[4] Jesus then added a verse from Leviticus: "And the second is like it: 'Love your neighbor as yourself.'"[5] For Christians, these two verses have become the Great Commandments of our faith.

If you look closely, you'll see that Jesus set up a triangle. Each side depends on the other two. You can't obey one part of this commandment without keeping the other two. You can't love God without loving your neighbors, and you can't love yourself without loving God, and you can't love your neighbors without loving God. In the great commandment, Jesus requires all three to be linked. To love God means to love yourself and to love your neighbor.

Like many of Jesus's sayings, the Great Commandments sound beautiful, even poetic. You want to cross-stitch them in a pretty design and hang them in a magnetic frame on your refrigerator door. Yes, they do sound beautiful…until you try to live them. Then the difficulty of trying to obey the commands in real life will twist your soul into a pretzel. In the book of Revelation, the angel told John to eat the scroll. He did, saying the scroll tasted like honey in his mouth. But when he swallowed it, it made him sick to his stomach.[6]

When you try to obey God, you find that it's far from poetry. It's more like eating something that doesn't agree with you. In your own strength you simply can't muster what it takes to love people. They are too hard to love. No matter how well-intentioned you are, people will soon drain your goodwill.

Have you ever made a New Year's resolution to be more loving? How long did that last? Fifteen minutes? I usually do all right until I drive somewhere, and as soon as someone using a cell phone creeps into my lane or cuts me off, well, let's just say I give up on that resolution. Whether our weak point is loving the crazy driver in traffic, or the neighbor who lets his dogs outside to bark at four in the morning, or a fellow church member who uses group prayer to spread gossip, we don't have hearts deep enough to love people without having God's love flowing through us to the other person.

Loving God, Loving Others

And that's the point. As we open our lives to the love of God in Christ, his love flows in us and through us. You cannot hold the ocean in a thimble, and our limited souls cannot contain the love of God. God is generous. He always sends more blessings than we can contain so that his love runs over, filling our lives and then spilling over into the lives of those closest to us. Our limited love for others is overwhelmed by God's love for the others. If we love God, we will love our brothers and sisters. If we don't love them, we don't love God. Jesus said the way the world would know we were his followers is by the way we love one another.[7]

If you love God with everything you have, sooner or later he will bring you someone who needs to be loved. Many people have a hard time believing God would love them because, frankly, no one else has. If their own parents or family members have not loved them, why would God? So God will bring you into their lives, and you will begin to love them. At first they will be hostile and resistant. Not knowing love when they see it, they will be suspicious of you. But God will not give up, and he won't let you give up. When the person asks why you are different, you can tell her about how Jesus has loved you and how Jesus wants to love her as well.

Loving people will drive you to love God more. But people being what they are, they'll drain your life of every ounce of energy. As we discussed earlier, we all are needy. And most of us look to others to fill our emptiness. So as you love others, you will be drained. Only God can restore what you give out, filling your emptiness and replenishing your strength as you pray to him and worship him. When you seek him and invite his presence, God will refill your life with his nearness. If you invite his Spirit to flow into your life, he will always answer that request.

With our lives filled with God's presence, we are free to love others without expectation or need of anything in return. We don't have to manipulate people into acting like the kind of people we think we need. We are free to allow our neighbors to be who they are. Feeling this freedom, friends usually relax and allow us the same freedom. We can be who we are without fear of being judged or manipulated. Jesus told his disciples not to limit their hospitality to friends who would later repay them with a reciprocal dinner invitation. I think love is the same way. I believe Jesus wants his followers to be sure to love those who cannot love back.

A Marriage of Two Healthy People

Can you imagine what a marriage would look like if it was based on the kind of generous love that expects nothing in return? The apostle Paul could, so he described this type of marriage. The Christians in Ephesus had sent Paul a letter, and based on Paul's letter back to them, their questions seem to have gone like this: "Okay, Paul, we're Christians. Now what?" Paul responded by reminding them of the essence of the gospel message (in Ephesians 1–3). Then, beginning in chapter 4, he told them, "In light of God's great love, live a life worthy of this calling." What follows is practical teaching on spiritual growth, dealing with anger, and family life.[8]

When Paul got to the marriage relationship, he framed it in terms of Christ's love for his church.[9] The witness of a Christian marriage tells much more than the story of two people loving each other. Somehow it makes known the very presence of Christ. Paul used a classic tool of rhetoric in approaching his subject. Because he knew he was bringing up a difficult topic in challenging husbands to love their wives, he began by writing to wives: "Wives, submit to your husbands!"[10] Paul's letter would have been read out loud in a public worship service. Every man in the service just then was elbowing his wife. "Honey, listen to this man. Paul really knows what he's talking about."

Once Paul had the husbands agreeing with him, the trap was set. "Husbands, love your wives," Paul wrote next.[11] That would have been welcomed, since no husband would express a problem with the idea of loving his wife. But Paul didn't stop there. He added a qualifier, and it's a killer: "Love as Christ loved the church."[12] The husband who had just told his wife to listen to Paul was caught. Love your wife in the same way Christ loved the church, Paul said. And husbands had to listen. After all, they had just told everyone how smart Paul was.

The husband, according to this teaching, is to approach his wife the same way Christ comes to the church. Christ loves the church because of who he is. He needs nothing from the church in return. He desires only the best for the church. What would happen if husbands approached their marriages this way? What if a husband looked at his wife without any thought of what he could get from her? Instead, what if husbands asked, "How does my wife need me to love her today? How can I help her become more of who Christ created her to be?"

In Genesis, Adam was placed in the garden to look after it and care for it. He understood his role as a steward.[13] A few verses later, God gave Eve to Adam. He would have understood immediately that he was to be a steward of Eve as well. The role of the steward is to maximize the value of his Master's investment. In the same way, Christian husbands are to be stewards of their wives. They are called to help identify and enhance whatever dreams and potential God placed in their wives at their creation. In this way, the husband loves his wife as Christ loves the church. This is a vastly different teaching from what we hear and see in every aspect of our culture. Christlike love, unlike the myth of the soul mate or the starry-eyed fluttering of the heart in romance, exists for the sake of the other.

When you know your "yes"—knowing you are treasured by the Father and have been called to a Kingdom purpose—then you can be free to love the other without any selfish motives or hidden agendas. Both partners are free to be who they are, knowing that they don't have to earn the other's love.

Loving the Unlovely

One side of the triangle found in the Great Commandments is to love our neighbors just as we love ourselves. We all know how easy it is to give ourselves a break. Even when we know what we said or did was wrong, privately thinking it over later, it's not difficult to go easy on ourselves. We were tired or rushed or had just finished a high-pressure day at work. We find ways to love ourselves even when we know we were in the wrong.

We know from highly personal experience that love can be extended to those who are not always model citizens—ourselves. But it's not easy to extend the same grace to others. Jesus commands us to love our neighbors. The problem is that the neighbors, for one reason or another, will often be people who are not quite to our liking. Jesus never draws such a distinction. According to his definition, a neighbor is *anyone* who needs love.

And it goes beyond that. In response to a lawyer's question, Jesus used a story to describe just what a neighbor is. After telling about a Samaritan stopping and helping a man attacked by robbers, when both a priest and a Levite had walked by the victim, Jesus asked the lawyer, "Which of these three do you think proved to be a neighbor to the man who fell among the thieves?" The lawyer correctly identified the Samaritan, who was the only one of the three passersby to stop and help. Then Jesus said, "Go and do likewise."[14]

Jesus was saying not only to love our neighbors but also to *be* neighbors to those in need. We are to love our neighbors, no matter how we feel toward them. But at the same time, we are to be neighbors to all who cross our paths and need help. More important than defining who are our neighbors, each of us should ask, "Am I a neighbor to those around me?"

FREE TO LOVE

What would happen if we were whole and complete in Christ and were able to love those whose needs are great and who cannot repay any of our love? For one thing, we would love freely and generously, understanding that giving love to others never diminishes us. We could celebrate with friends and truly enjoy their successes, understanding that their victories do not take anything away from us.

We would be quick to find moments when we could serve others. We would quiet our lives in order to be more aware of those around us and how we might meet their needs. How often do we miss seeing the ways Christ wants us to love others?

We would love others without first demanding that they conform to our requirements or somehow become acceptable to us. We would not be in competition with anyone else, feeling pressure to look better than we are or hurrying so we'll be first in line to get a reward. God has plenty of blessings for all his children, and he will still have blessings left to give away whenever we get there. God's being good to someone else doesn't mean he will have nothing left to give us later on.

When we learn this, we can love God with everything we are; we can love ourselves and love our neighbors the way we love God. When this happens, we keep the Great Commandments. We are then living in the "yes" of Christ, and we can freely share his "yes" with everyone he brings to us to love.

The "Yes" of Simplicity

God's "yes" frees us from the tyranny of things

I am not saying this because I am in need, for I have
learned to be content whatever the circumstances.

—PAUL (PHILIPPIANS 4:11)

A s I write this chapter, politicians are meeting to try to find a way to
jump-start the nation's struggling economy. The United States has
not yet found a way out of the "Great Recession" that started in 2008.
Signs of impending economic collapse were visible before then, but as
President Bush's economic team prepared to hand over the reins of government to President Obama and his economic team in the fall of 2008,
it became evident that the entire financial system of the United States was
in danger of collapsing. In hindsight, we should have been more fright-
ened than we were. The American public has since learned how close we
came to a complete economic meltdown.

THE MELTDOWN

While I make no claims to being an economist, here is what seems to
have happened. In 2007 the financial sector had become the center of
wealth creation in our economy. More than 40 percent of corporate profits

in 2007 came from this sector.[1] The mortgage industry was the fuel that kept this engine running, and a number of factors created a liquidity bubble. A lot of people had money to invest, and they invested in the housing market. These investments were sold using financial instruments that were so complex most people could not understand them, not even the CEOs of the companies that sold them.[2] Because the investments so generously rewarded those who sold them, increasingly more of these financial packages were sold. And to feed the investment machine, more houses had to be sold.

Mortgage companies started offering loans for the full value of a home. In some cases home-equity loans were built into the original mortgage to allow the prospective homeowner to borrow up to 125 percent of the home's value. Homebuyers used the extra cash to purchase boats, cars, and furniture or to pay for vacations.[3] What is even more surprising, mortgage lenders required little or no documentation to prove the borrowers had the ability to repay the loans. Loan standards weren't just lowered; they were dropped altogether.[4] This financial house of cards was built on the assumption that home values would always go up, so if some borrowers defaulted on their loans, the amount borrowed would be recoverable through the equity built up in the homes.

That was the flaw in the logic. The housing market did not continue to rise as it had in the previous years. In fact, in 2007 the housing market started to collapse. Houses that had been used as collateral for home-equity loans and low-interest adjustable mortgages were no longer worth the amount that had been borrowed against them. Buyers were "upside-down"—they now owed more than the house was worth. Many homes slipped into foreclosure. Construction of new homes slowed nearly to a stop. Builders couldn't find money to finance construction projects. Banks stopped lending. People stopped buying. Workers were laid off, manufacturing plants closed, and banks failed. The housing bubble had burst, and with its collapse, the entire economy of the United States was almost brought down. The more we find out about the Great Recession, the more we understand how close we came to another Great Depression.

The irony of all this is that the crisis could have been prevented. I don't mean just that knowledgeable people should have read the danger signs and blown the whistle. I am talking about *all* of us. We all had a part in the economic meltdown. It was driven by greed. Americans willingly took advantage of loan offers that required no down payment and that had initially low interest rates so they could buy houses they couldn't afford. Beyond that, home-equity loans were used to pay for luxury items that didn't hold their value, much less appreciate. This put homeowners further in debt, and when the bubble burst, they couldn't pay back what they owed.

Banks, making record profits on fees and finance charges, encouraged people to go deeper in debt. They based this approach on the principle of using other people's money. As a result, lines of credit were opened to anyone holding a mortgage. Greed went unchecked because most government regulation of the financial industry had been lifted. Applying for a loan was about as easy as renting a movie from Netflix.

In escalating numbers, people were experiencing the American dream of buying their own homes, and in the freewheeling financial climate, they were taking out loans on more expensive homes than they would have considered just a few years earlier. This encouraged lending agencies to increase the amount of money they made available for loans. When overstretched consumers couldn't continue to make mortgage payments, the system collapsed. This happened because people and organizations, including governments, were unwilling to live within their means. Easy credit meant people were spending money they didn't have. When the loans had to be repaid, including mortgages, auto loans, and other consumer credit, people were in so deep they had no hope of paying their debts. As a nation, we will be unraveling the consequences of this recklessness for years to come.

THE NEED THAT DRIVES GREED

In our culture, a person's status is determined by what he possesses. We have to have the newest electronic gadgets, the latest car, an apartment in the trendiest building. The list of "must haves" is constantly changing, updated, and revised. Just staying up with what is in and what is out is almost a full-time job. And the things we "must" have aren't free. Marketers work hard to make us dissatisfied with our lot in life, not as a public service, but because they want to sell us more stuff. They profit only when they succeed in convincing us to spend more money. Our entire economy depends on consumers spending more money, even money we don't have.

The deeper irony of almost spending ourselves into oblivion is that we aren't any happier. The demands of our 24/7 world have left us stressed out, worn-out, and very lonely. For all the hype about social networking, we have actually become more isolated. When I was a teenager, getting a new LP (yeah, a large black vinyl record album) was a community event. You would call your friends, and everyone would meet at the house with the best stereo, and we would listen to the album together. We would discover new songs and new artists together. We would read the liner notes and study the album's cover art to see if there were any hidden messages to be deciphered. We would do all this with a group of friends, and the music became one of the things that cemented our friendship.

Now young people download the latest music from a website onto a personal listening device, then put in their earplugs. With this system, listening to music becomes a solitary experience. The act of putting in earplugs tells the world the person doesn't want to be engaged in conversation. Music has evolved from a communal bonding experience to an individual pursuit.

This loneliness has led to the development of more gadgets to help us stay connected with people. Internet video conferencing, smartphones, instant messaging, Twitter—each with its own software and hardware requirements and, of course, more fees. Our frantic efforts to prove our value as persons and establish our identities as "brands" has driven us to our physical, emotional, psychological, and financial limits. (I find it interesting that successful people are those who have established their "brands" through the effective use of social media. That is, they have become commodities, merchandise items that can be sold and marketed. They collect fans and followers. They compare the number of friends they have on Facebook against the friends lists of their actual friends. They are no longer celebrated as people but as brands.)

This kind of success has left most of us unsatisfied. This dissatisfaction, the opposite of contentment, is universally experienced but not uniformly addressed. Not everyone believes that more and better possessions will quiet their disquiet. But many of us do believe that lie, and we keep spending money to collect more possessions and have the latest gadgets to prove our value, and on it goes. Seen in this light, it's not hard to understand how greed and discontent led to the financial collapse of 2008.

In August 2010 the headline article of the *New York Times* business section was "But Will It Make You Happy?" The question asked by the article's writer, Stephanie Rosenbloom, was this: Was the stuff you were buying worth all the long hours you had to work and the sacrifices that longer hours of work required of you? Rosenbloom followed a number of young professionals who had given a negative answer to that question. A young professional woman, who earlier in the article complained of being on a "work-spend treadmill," provided the article's final quote: "Give away some of your stuff. See how it feels."[5]

Not only is our manic consumerism taking a devastating toll on our individual lives and our families, but our consumerism has also resulted in damaging the environment. I don't propose to debate the issue of global warming, but there is growing evidence that our lifestyles are no longer sustainable on several levels. Right now, the rising price of oil has caused hardships for most middle-class families in America. Food costs continue to rise as well. Urban sprawl means a lot of us have moved farther from the places we work and, thus, have to endure longer commutes, which are costly in terms of money, time, stress, and damage to relationships.

One issue builds on another. For instance, as we demand more stuff, manufacturing uses more of the earth's resources. A ballooning population means more people are demanding more stuff. Scientific journals regularly publish articles discussing the growing shortage of fresh water. The oceans are overfished to keep up with the world's appetite. The point is obvious, even to a Baptist preacher: we could make a dramatic impact on the care of our world if we simply stopped buying so much stuff. A relatively easy starting place is to stop buying stuff we don't need.

Our addiction to stuff is costing us more in our personal lives. I can remember when computers were introduced as timesaving devices! Yes, computers do allow us to do certain things more quickly. But now, instead of having more leisure time, we are required to do more work so that the efficiencies made possible by technology are paying the greatest dividends in productivity. Most of us spend more time at work, not less, than we did ten years ago. The digital age means greater numbers of us can work from home, but it also means we have more difficulty turning work off. Smartphones that handle our e-mail, contacts, documents, and schedules also mean our employers may expect access to us twenty-four hours a day, seven days a week.

ENOUGH

In the middle of the economic crisis, I was browsing a local bookstore and noticed a book on the new-releases stack. The book was called *Enough,* by John Bogle. As a pastor, I often preach about contentment. And I have to admit my surprise when I noticed that Bogle, who is the founder of the Vanguard Group, a champion of capitalism, wrote a book saying that in our rush to enjoy the good life, we have missed everything that makes life good. When those who are winning the game say the game isn't worth what it costs to play, we need to listen.

Bogle wrote:

What *are* the things by which we should measure our lives?
I'm still searching for the ultimate answer to that question.
But I know that we can never let things as such—the material
possessions we may come to accumulate—become the measure
of our lives.... Such a measure is absurd; it is superficial; and,
finally, it is self-defeating.[6]

Self-defeating? That is an interesting observation from someone who
is regarded as one of the most successful men in America. Yet in his book
he makes the same point Jesus once made: "What good will it be for
someone to gain the whole world, yet forfeit their soul? Or what can
anyone give in exchange for their soul?"[7]

We mistakenly think that if one thing can't make us happy, we simply haven't bought the right thing. We need to shop at another store to
find just the right new thing. When we find the treasured possession, we
will be happy. But then the newness wears off, and we buy something
else. This cycle, of course, is nothing new, and that is part of the problem.
We should know better. But no matter how hard we try (maybe I should
say, "No matter how much we talk about trying"), we can't seem to free
ourselves from the cycle of discontent. In Tennessee Williams's play *Cat
on a Hot Tin Roof,* Big Daddy exclaims, "The human animal is a beast
that...buys and buys and...has the crazy hope that one of his purchases
will be life everlasting!—Which it never can be."[8]

Tennessee Williams was right. You can't buy eternal life, or happiness, or love, or anything else that makes life worth living. Piling up more
possessions might provide a temporary distraction and deliver short-term
pleasure, but sooner or later the new wears off everything, and then you
are unsatisfied again. When your discontent returns, it's almost guaranteed that you will buy something else. Charge it on your credit card;
take another draw against your home equity; open another account. We

are experts at deceiving ourselves. We tell ourselves we will pay it all off somehow.

Sadly, we rarely connect the dots and stop buying things we don't need and can't afford so that we can live within our means and regain peace of mind. We choose to believe instead that the next high will fix us.

FINDING MARGIN

Here again, the church doesn't help much. While the world says you can buy eternal life (and you can't), the church sends a mixed message that you can earn eternal life (you can't). All our efforts to prove ourselves worthy of God's love are self-defeating, but we don't want to face that fact. It's hard for us to understand and accept without question the meaning of "God's free gift of salvation." Perhaps pride keeps us from accepting that we are not worthy of God's love, and, on top of that, we can't do anything to make ourselves more deserving. It's all about God. He loves us because that's who he is. It's called grace.

A few years ago we did a programming audit of our church's ministries. We constructed a chart of all the times we invited our members to do something, what age group was targeted by the program, and what would be required to be involved in that program. We were shocked by what we discovered. While we claim to be a pro-family church, we were in reality working against families. We were bringing parents to church for one meeting. Then the parents would need to bring their children back to the church for another meeting. If parents and children were fully involved in every church opportunity available, they would have never been home together on any night of the week.

This was eye-opening. Our church revamped the entire weekly program schedule to better coordinate the involvement of parents and their children.

Dr. Richard Swenson was one of the first people to address this issue from a faith perspective. In his book *Margin,* he pointed out that people become so stressed in every area of life that they no longer have the margin—the excess capacity of time and emotional, psychological, and financial resources—to respond to unexpected challenges. A child has a cold and can't go to school. This means one of the working parents has to stay home and care for the sick child. Depending on each parent's work situation, staying home one day may have significant financial implications on the family. This, of course, introduces another level of stress. And even if there are no financial implications, the parent is still stressed by missing a day of work and now being further behind on assignments. This is just one example. Swenson's point is we are so maxed out that we simply don't have the necessary capacities to live the lives we desire. Yes, others have had it harder, but as Swenson notes, "Never before have people faced the particular constellations of factors which today are plotting together for our misery."[9]

WINNING THE WRONG RACE

Lily Tomlin, the famous comedienne, once said, "The problem with the rat race is that even if you win, you are still a rat."[10] What if we, as Christ-followers, began to understand that being in the rat race works directly against our "yes" from God? What if we understood that the American way of life shouts a "no" in the face of Christ's "yes"? What if we decided we would no longer allow possessions to define our identities and meaning? What if we asked the core question: What do I *really* need to live a good life? And then answered it honestly? What if we carried out a thorough and honest inventory of our needs and adjusted our possessions and living situations to meet those actual needs?

I am not advocating a move to asceticism or puritan austerity, but most of us could simplify our lives and still live way above the average standard of living. How many pairs of shoes do you need? How many computers? phones? cars? How big a house? How much freedom could you add to your life if you reduced the amount of stuff you have to take care of? Get rid of the clutter; you'll have less to clean, less to keep track of, less to maintain and repair and put away after it's used. Is there another country on earth that would have a television show called *Clean House: Search for the Messiest Home in the Country*?

One of the saddest stories in the New Testament is the one of the rich young ruler. At least it was sad for Jesus. When the man walked away from Jesus, we see Jesus honestly grieve the young man's decision. While we do not know exactly what was going on inside the young man, we are given enough clues to draw some conclusions. We are told his countenance fell. We don't know if his smile went to a frown or if he simply slumped his shoulders. We know from the reports of those standing nearby that Jesus had just asked him for the one thing he couldn't give. We also are told that he had great wealth. Divesting himself of his wealth was not what he thought would be required. The cost of following Jesus was just too high.[11]

And yet Jesus extended the same invitation to this man that he had given the original Twelve. Peter and the rest of the disciples had been called to leave everything and come follow Jesus. The rich young ruler was given an offer to be the thirteenth disciple, but his stuff wouldn't let him go. He would not be the last person caught in that trap.

Popular radio and television personality Dave Ramsey has become nationally known for helping people deal with personal debt. Our desire to have all the material things that define the so-called good life has put us in bondage to our things. As a result, our lives have become virtual prisons. We can't do what we want to do because we have to think first about taking care of our possessions.

Among the Millennials there is a movement back to simplicity. Disillusioned by the materialism of the Boomers and disappointed in the downward slide of economic expectations (they are the first generation in America that has no expectation of doing better than their parents), today's young adults are simply stepping out of the rat race. They have different expectations of their jobs, which frees them to expand the scope of what they will do with their lives. They are putting off marriage until later and having children later. They seem to be in no hurry to embrace a form of "responsible, profitable adulthood" that resembles the life of their parents.

There is a new freedom in this simplicity. Why wouldn't there be? If our sense of worth and purpose is no longer defined by stuff, we are free to live without unnecessary complications. Not only do we have more of a margin in life, but we also are free to be more generous. The information revolution has meant the mainstream media no longer control information, and more people can access virtually unlimited information on their own. Now we are more aware of the suffering in Darfur and the continuing agony in Haiti. The Internet not only allows us to know about these things; it also means we can organize significant responses to meet human needs. Living simply means you have more to give to a world that is suffering.

The "yes" of Jesus allows us to live from the inside out. We are neither defined nor held captive by our possessions, but rather we are known for who we are in Christ. Possessions lose their power to control us.

Jesus is our model of how to live life to its fullest, and he lived simply. He walked everywhere. He didn't own a home. He depended on the generosity of friends for the basics of life. Yet he was rich in the things that matter: an intimate relationship with God the Father and rich, growing relationships with his friends. But it's not a lack of information that keeps us from following this path, is it?

Shane Claiborne has become a modern-day prophet whose message of radical discipleship is challenging the status quo of the North American church. Claiborne and his friends have embraced a lifestyle of radical simplicity, even poverty. So much so, some call them New Monastics. Raised in East Tennessee in an area "suffocated by Christianity," he has rejected the consumerism of American evangelicalism. Claiborne speaks and writes books challenging the church to examine its values and assumptions. Should the Christian community champion consumerism and capitalism?[12]

Claiborne has written about his Christian conversion, recalling that everyone talked to him about what to believe, "but no one had told me how Christians live."[13] Eager to be a good disciple, he bought more stuff.[14] Only this time he was buying "Jesus stuff": T-shirts, bumper stickers, music. He and a friend began reading the Bible to see if Jesus had any answers for their basic questions. They were surprised by what they found out. The more they read, the more they understood that a lot of American consumerism directly contradicts the teachings of Jesus. The result of his study was the founding of The Simple Way, a Christian community in Philadelphia.

He went to India on one of his first mission trips and was deeply moved by the lepers he encountered. He was surprised to learn leprosy is a disease of the nerves. Without a proper sense of touch, wounds are left untreated, and the skin sloughs off. Claiborne suggests Christians have become numb, like the lepers he helped. He is calling on us to regain our feeling, our spiritual sense of touch, by reconnecting with Jesus at a much deeper level.[15]

Claiborne isn't the only one to make this discovery. Successful corporate executives are discovering similar things. Richard Stearns was CEO of an international corporation. His life included international travel, houses, and cars. Daily luxuries were wrapped up in his comfortable Christianity. Then, similar to Claiborne, he took a mission trip that began to unravel his world. Stearns eventually left his corporate position to become president of World Vision. In his book *The Hole in Our Gospel,* he wrote:

There is a real problem with this limited view of the kingdom of God; it is not the whole gospel. Instead, it's a gospel with a gaping hole. First, focusing almost exclusively on the afterlife reduces the importance of what God expects of us in this life. The kingdom of God, which Christ said is "within you" (Luke 17:21 NKJV), was intended to change and challenge everything in our fallen world in the here and now. It was not meant to be a way to leave the world but rather the means to actually redeem it.[16]

Beginning with a quote from his former pastor, Gary Gulbranson, "It's not what you believe that counts; it's what you believe enough to do,"[17] Stearns challenges the church to reclaim the full gospel of Christ, to use the identity and destiny of our "yes" to join Christ on his Father-sent mission to redeem the world. Again, Stearns wrote:

> This *whole gospel* [emphasis added] is truly good news for the poor, and it is the foundation for a social revolution that has the power to change the world. And if this was Jesus' mission, it is also the mission of all who claim to follow Him. It is my mission, it is your mission, and it is the mission of the Church.[18]

More than I would like to admit, Claiborne's and Stearns's messages are aimed right at me. A lot of what they say is right. I use too much, buy too much, consume too much. And all of this "too much" hurts the earth and other people. And in the end, it hurts me.

So why don't I live in the freedom I claim Christ gives me? Simple. I have to face the hard truth that in a lot of ways I am not completely convinced of the message of the gospel. I don't believe that my value as a person is secure in Christ's love for me. I don't believe that he chose to love me before I knew anything about him. I can't believe that before I ever existed, God held me in his heart and that he has held me in it ever since. I can't believe that his grace to me is just given to me, freely, and that no matter how hard I try, I can't do a single thing to deserve it. Paul reminds us, "Everything that does not come from faith is sin."[19] I am not sure our complicated, complex, and consumer-driven lives are centered in our faith in Christ. And because these things don't come from faith, according to Paul that makes them sin.

While I am not there yet, I am doing better. Sometimes I catch myself pushing a little too hard because I still think God's love for me relies on how much I accomplish, how productive I am, how many things I can report that I did for him. I still battle the lingering conviction that somehow I can do things to justify his love.

One day I will understand that, like the universe itself, God's love just is. I can't fully grasp it or understand it. I can only accept it, only receive it. And then live in the joyful freedom this glorious truth brings me. On that day I will at last be free. And not just me but all those who finally understand the words of the children's hymn:

> Jesus loves me! This I know,
> For the Bible tells me so;
> Little ones to Him belong;
> They are weak, but He is strong.
> Yes, Jesus loves me!
> Yes, Jesus loves me!
> Yes, Jesus loves me!
> The Bible tells me so.[20]

One "Yes" Does Not Fit All

Your "yes" is unique.
You can't live someone else's.

When Peter saw him [the apostle John], he said to Jesus, "Lord—what about him?" "If I want him to remain until I come," Jesus answered, "what is that to you? As for you, follow Me."

—JOHN 21:21–22, HCSB

The magazine ad read, "One size fits all." It didn't. The robe I ordered was too short, and I hate a robe that is too short. Since I'm over six feet tall, it's hard to find robes that fit me well, and this one was guaranteed to fit. But it didn't. What it did do was make me look silly. One size does not fit all. I guess I shouldn't have been surprised.

No matter what we are considering—a new bathrobe or the best way to be involved in ministry—one size never fits us all. People are too different, each unique. Each of us is a one-of-a-kind compilation of numerous possibilities. Jesus Christ, in whom all things hold together, understands this. He is the One who made each of us unique. And his relationship with each of us is as unique as we are.

Again, our culture is at odds with this reality. Our world demands standardization, because it increases efficiency and holds down costs. So rule makers and manufacturers and those who control what is said and not said on mass media outlets aim for a mythical "conglomerate human." The result is an expectation of uniformity. We are required to do certain things the same way every time. Policies are written in such a way that managers will make the same decisions in the same situations every time. This reduces the likelihood of surprises and cuts down on the amount of time spent in thinking creatively. Adherence to an entrenched way of doing things increases efficiency, but it does nothing for innovation, progress, or outthinking the competition. And it fails to reflect the reality of everyday life.

One point of contention between Baby Boom corporate managers and Gen Y employees is the younger generation's resistance to working within the same parameters as everyone else.[1] Gen Y workers want flexible work hours and limited oversight, but they also desire a good deal of personal support from supervisors. They will get the work done but in their way and their time. Usually they are creative and energetic in their approach to solving problems. But their approaches are not likely to track closely with established corporate practice. As frustrating as this can be for Boomer managers, each Gen Y employee is as unique as a snowflake. An individual's uniqueness reflects the realities of how we are made, but it is not a high value when the goal is to maximize corporate efficiency.

A Unique You

The generations that follow the Boomers resist social structures, including career tracks, that are dictated by someone else. Likewise, they resist any spiritual program or process that can't be easily adapted to their particular needs. I happen to be on their side on this one. It's easy for religious leaders to develop a greater allegiance to traditions or points of doctrine than to the heart of the gospel message. For some, the insistence on uniformity of religious practice is an attempt to achieve unity. But it's a mistake to think that uniformity will bring about unity. The two are not the same.

What unifies us as believers is our shared relationship with Jesus Christ, not the protocol of a particular discipleship process. Each experience will be unique because each person is unique, and the uniqueness of each relationship reveals a unique aspect of Jesus. With each follower of Jesus bringing her revelation of Christ to the body, the church is given a more accurate and beautiful portrait of Christ.

But it can frustrate church leaders when every believer is having a unique experience with the Lord. Church leaders like to find something that works and then duplicate it. (Some critics have compared this to the speed and efficiency that resulted when Henry Ford began manufacturing Model Ts using interchangeable parts and mass production.) But it's a mistake to think that Christians who seek to grow spiritually are interchangeable. What has worked in one church in North America will not necessarily work in any other church. Not only does one size *not* fit all, but one-size programs rarely transfer well to other settings or communities. Every church, like every believer, is meant to present a unique expression of a living relationship with Christ.

Pressuring others to conform to an experience of Christ that is considered "normative" for Christians is not helpful. For generations, the experience of the apostle Paul on the road to Damascus was held up as the norm. If a person had a conversion experience, it had to be dramatic, or it was suspect. The blinding flash of light and the voice of Jesus confronting the zealot Saul became the standard by which all conversions were measured. While his encounter with Christ was considered miraculous at the time, in past decades it was assumed that a real conversion would be accompanied by similar experiences.

It's easy to see the problem with this. Not everyone has a dramatic experience. I didn't. I was loved into the Kingdom of God. Everyone I knew was a believer. Everyone talked about Jesus. For me, deciding to follow Jesus was as natural as breathing. There has never been a time in my life when I was not aware of him. And when I reached a certain age, I realized my relationship with Christ was somehow outside the parameters of an "acceptable" Christian testimony.

For years I felt I had been cheated because my story was not dramatic. Only later did I understand how blessed I was to grow up in a loving Christian family. My experience with Christ was uniquely tailored to who I am. Christ spoke to me, aware of the person I am and how I needed to hear from him. The Christians I knew were loving, committed, sincere, real people. Why wouldn't I want to follow their Lord?

Some of you grew up in the faith, and others didn't. Some of you drifted from your spiritual roots, and it was years before you came back home. Others started out far from God and gradually, through dramatic and even miraculous circumstances, came to know God in a very real way. Every story is different, and it makes no sense to expect a person's introduction to saving faith to follow a preapproved script. You are not Paul, and you are not me. But the one thing we have in common—Paul, you, and me, and every other believer—is our love for Jesus.

Conversion stories in the Bible are as different as the people who are being called by God. Abraham was a pagan enjoying a comfortable life in Ur. David was a courageous, though young and not physically impressive, sheepherder. Moses was a murderer. Ruth was a Gentile whose heart was more sincere than just about any other person's in Scripture. At the risk of losing her life, Esther stood up to a king to save God's people from genocide. Rahab was a prostitute, Zacchaeus was a liar and a cheater, Peter a hothead, and John a loyal, dedicated, unwavering follower of Jesus.

Not everyone can conform to the norm. I couldn't. I never did fit in, not in college or later in seminary. I was so different from my classmates that I wondered if I had made a mistake going into the ministry. One day as I walked across campus at Southern Seminary in Louisville, Kentucky, Bill Leonard, a professor of church history, stopped to talk. This made me nervous. Before then, if a professor had stopped me on campus, it was because I was in trouble. But I wasn't in trouble. In fact, Dr. Leonard wanted to know a little more about me—where I had grown up, what I wanted to do with my degree, all about my family. He was genuinely interested in me as a person.

Just as we were saying good-bye, he added, "You are a very unique person on our campus." He must have seen the shame on my face. I knew I was unique, and it wasn't all that much fun. He patted me on the shoulder as he continued, "I pray you don't lose that. It's Christ's gift to his church."

As far as I can remember, that was the first time anyone had confirmed my uniqueness and seen it as a positive! After hearing from my professor, I began to understand why I didn't fit the norm. I was never supposed to fit. I was supposed to understand who I was in Christ and express my uniqueness as a blessing from Christ through which he would reveal himself to his church and the world.

My uniqueness reveals something of Christ that no one else does. Like a little piece of glass in a stained-glass window, I reflect and refract light from God's glory in a way that nobody else can. I finally began to understand that just as Jesus had created me as a unique individual, Jesus would love me uniquely. While my experience would share large swaths in common with Christians around the world and across time, many moments of this relationship would be just my own. The Shepherd knows his sheep, and his sheep know him.

JUST FOR YOU

There is one size that fits you and one size that fits me. God offers his "yes" to each of us, but no one can point you to your "yes." You have to find it in your own journey. The Spirit calls, and you follow him along a road meant only for you. Why? Because Christ wants to show you things that are there for you alone. In geometry you start to solve a problem by examining the givens of the problem. Each problem has a unique set of givens. The same is true of people. We each have a unique set of gifts, passions, talents, and experiences. Your "yes" from Christ will take into consideration and take full advantage of every aspect of your self.

We know that each of our children is different. My wife and I have twin sons, and although the doctor told us they are fraternal twins, we have long suspected they are identical. They look enough alike to fool their friends, but they are very different. Each one requires a unique touch to match his personality. So why are we surprised that we get treated differently by the Father? Because each of us is unique, we need to be loved in a way that takes into account our uniqueness.

One of my sons is very sensitive, and if you correct him, he is wounded to the core. He will worry for the rest of the day that you are still mad at him. As parents, my wife and I learned to be very careful how we dealt with him. Our other son has never admitted being wrong...yet! If we punished him, he suffered the punishment like a political prisoner. He would serve the time, but never did he admit the crime. His attitude always indicated that we would one day realize we were wrong to hold him responsible for the misdeed in question.

We love both sons more than I can express. They continue to be sources of great joy to us. But they require very different approaches from us.

I think this is one of the points Jesus was making when he said, "My sheep listen to my voice; I know them, and they follow me."[2] Jesus knows what makes us tick, the things that frustrate and delight us, everything about us. He knows how to deal with each of us in ways that are best for us as individuals. We would expect this from a good earthly father. Why would we be surprised to find that God is such a perceptive and attentive Father?

When word got out in the Israelite camp that a young shepherd by the name of David had accepted the challenge of the Philistine giant, Goliath, King Saul summoned David to his tent. After finding out more about David, Saul told him to wear the king's armor into combat. The king's men dressed the young shepherd in the king's armor, and that must have been a sight. Saul stood a head taller than everyone else in Israel. That was one of the reasons he was chosen to be king. David was, well, smaller. The armor must have swallowed him. Wisely, David politely refused the king's offer and chose to fight Goliath the same way he fought off wild animals that had attacked his sheep. David had the courage to trust the way God had made him and had worked in him in the past. God had given him mobility and quickness, as well as a deadly aim with a slingshot. David would not have won against the giant if he had been hampered by a heavy, cumbersome suit of armor. David had to follow God in a way that fit him.[3]

Most parents are familiar with the verse in Proverbs that tells us to "start children off on the way they should go, and even when they are old they will not turn from it."[4] Most parents focus on the phrase "on the way the child should go" and work hard to make sure their children know the way of the Lord. We drill our children with facts, having them learn creeds and helping them memorize Bible verses. We emphasize the right information, seeking to instruct them in the "way they should go." Don't misunderstand me; I encourage parents to take responsibility for the religious education of their children. But what if we took the emphasis off "the way" and instead focused on the child? What if instead of reading the verse "the *way* the child should go," we read it "the way the *child* should go"?

The difference is profound.

Parents should be charged with paying attention to the child and coaxing out the adult that God has placed in the child. There is no manual on this. There aren't "Six Steps to Success in Parenting" that cover the uniqueness of your child. It takes hours and hours, even years, of loving observation, interaction, and relationship. When parents focus on the child and not on a particular way, they encourage, provide feedback, and call out his uniqueness, linking who he is to God's calling in the child's life. Through this process children become confident in the people they were created to be and the purposes to which they are called. Their parents help them find their identity in Christ as well as their destiny in him.

THE HARD WORK OF "YES"

Because we are unique individuals, and because God speaks to us in ways that vary from "the norm," it's easy to wonder if we're really hearing from God. Most of us would rather fit in by sticking with a predetermined, regulation way of hearing God. We learned in junior high school that sticking out invites ridicule. So we are tempted to trade away what is unique about ourselves in exchange for the safety of the crowd.

But Christ did not call you to be someone else; he called you to be yourself and to follow him as you do that. Your true self cannot be revealed in any way other than in following Christ, learning from him, and engaging in long conversations with him.

Bible teachers often point out that leading rabbis in first-century Israel became known among the people, and those who wanted to be their disciples came to them and, in a sense, applied for the honor of being followers. But Jesus reversed that process by going out and inviting certain people to be his disciples. "Come, follow me," he said to fishermen, a tax collector, a zealot, and others.[5]

But why did Jesus call the Twelve away from their occupations? For one very basic reason: Jesus was on the move, and following him meant being on the move with him. Jesus and the disciples had hours of long, unhurried conversations as they traveled on foot around Galilee. These long conversations between the Teacher and his disciples happen for us in prayer and Bible study. This is the only place we can find our true selves. Maybe *find* is not the right word, for the true self isn't so much lost as it is hidden or dormant. That's why the miracle of the resurrection rings true for us. For us to come alive, Jesus, the resurrected One, must call us to life.

Jesus said, "To find your life you have to lose it."[6] We usually apply that truth to the sacrifice that is required of a disciple. In order to follow Jesus, you have to let go of your own agenda and submit to his lordship over every aspect of your life. But the same truth applies to the process of finding your true identity in Christ. You put away the illusions and distortions of your old self, built up by false messages from our culture, plus the expectations of your family and the advice of well-meaning friends. Everyone seems to have an opinion on how we ought to live our lives. If we are not careful, the small inner voice of the Spirit will be shouted down by the mob of opinions competing for our attention.

Most of us cave in to the culture's pressure, choosing to stop rowing against the current and just to drift wherever life will take us. These are the lives of quiet desperation that Henry David Thoreau noted so long ago.[7] Others choose to model their lives after people they respect or even idolize. But God doesn't want us to try to replicate our heroes. When we do, we're like bad Elvis impersonators who can't carry a tune. By following outside influences, we take on a life that does not fit who we were made to be.

Or worse, with the aid of the Internet, we can take on a life that isn't ours at all. Discussing his research into the new phenomenon of Internet addiction, Dr. Elias Aboujaoude wrote in *Virtually You: The Dangerous Powers of the E-Personality:*

> The way we see and evaluate ourselves is changing as a function of new personality traits born and nurtured in the virtual world. These include an exaggerated sense of our abilities, a superior attitude toward others, a new moral code that we adopt online, a proneness to impulsive behavior, and a tendency to regress to childlike states when faced with an open browser. Together, these traits combine into a "whole new you."[8]

He notes that, while online, people are more aggressive, more impulsive, and less concerned with consequences than they are in their real lives. Quoting psychologist Dr. John Suler, Aboujaoude says that the anonymity of the Internet can cause us to think that "those online behaviors 'aren't me at all.'" And if they aren't me, then we are not responsible for their consequences, so we can allow ourselves to engage in these behaviors with abandon.[9] In worst-case scenarios, the addiction gets to the point that we prefer our virtual lives to our real lives. "Our lives as we have known them, with our in-between IQs, so-so jobs, and bodies that leave something to be desired, now become boring in comparison with the online lives we have built."[10]

How sad is this? As adults we become so enamored by our pretend lives that we stop living our real lives. But Christ didn't come to give us a virtual "yes."

THE BEST "YES"

But for those who have the courage to walk with Christ and trust his answers for their identity and destiny, for those who reject the false selves pushed on them by our culture, there awaits a life lived in the synergy of grace. Athletes talk about being in the zone. Artists talk about being in the flow. It's the moment when you lose awareness of yourself and become immersed in the experience. You know where the ball is going to be. You see everything better, and you react faster. There seems to be no disconnect between what you are thinking and what you are doing. This is the life we are called to live. This is the "yes" of Christ—to become so aligned with the heart and mind of Christ that his thoughts are now your thoughts and his desires, your desires. Your life is magnified in the energy of Christ's life in you.

There is another aspect to the "yes" of Christ that sometimes puzzles us. Just as one size doesn't fit all, we don't find our "yes" just once. Our "yes" will change, deepen, expand, and morph throughout our lives. There are several reasons for this. First, we change, and our experiences with Christ change with us. When I was a little boy, I thought God had a radar system. My father worked at Redstone Arsenal, where he taught soldiers about the radar component in the army's missile systems. I thought radar was the coolest thing I had ever seen. It made sense to my young mind that if my father had a cool radar, then God must have a radar too, only his would be much bigger. My parents still talk about the Sunday school teacher who asked my class what we had learned about God, and I proudly announced that God had radars.

That image of God worked for me when I was little, but as I grew up, I had to let go of that understanding. Over the years I've had to let go of a lot of concepts of God that proved too small to contain the God I was trying to follow. As I have grown, my understanding has grown. While the essence of my understanding may stay the same, it has deepened. I compare it to looking at a childhood photo of someone who is now an adult. You can see a resemblance but not much. Over the years I have changed, and thus my experience with Christ has changed. The essence is still there, but most everything else about it has changed.

Second, the circumstances of our lives change. Life happens. God adapts his will in response to our choices and the choices made by others. His ultimate will doesn't change, but I believe God works in our moments to best accomplish his will with what we give him.

I have a friend who is a pastor in a nearby city. He had pastored churches for most of his career but then left parish ministry to teach at a college. When the church he now serves went through some painful transitions, they called my friend to serve as interim pastor. After he had spent two years walking them through a healing process, they called him as pastor. He confessed to me later that he had never thought it would be God's will that he serve as a church pastor again. "Maybe it wasn't," I said. But I am sure it wasn't God's will for the church to go through all it went through. Maybe God said, "I have a hurting church, and I know just the person to send." Today both that congregation and my friend are doing very well.

One day my executive assistant, Diane Mayfield, and I were talking about where we were raised. I grew up in just one town, Huntsville, Alabama. Mom and Dad moved there when I was five, and we never lived anywhere else. In fact, Mom and Dad still live there. Not Diane though. She is from a little bit of everywhere. Her father was always getting a new job. Listening to her describe her growing-up years, it seemed so foreign to me. But what a story it is.

Walter Mays started working for Ford in Dallas, where his hard work and natural skills set him apart. He was promoted and sent to Chicago and soon moved from there to find more opportunities at a production plant in Ohio. But Walter realized his Christian beliefs conflicted with the expectations he faced from the office. Eventually he was transferred to Detroit, where he left Ford. After being out of work for several months, Walter was contacted by a friend and ended up taking a job with LeTourneau, a manufacturing company in Longview, Texas. He restructured the company, and the resulting success attracted the attention of Marathon Oil, which bought out LeTourneau. In the transition, as with most buyouts, Walter was let go.

Now what? There was another "yes," unexpected and unique. Most of God's "yeses" end up being something you had never thought about but would have wanted had you known it was even possible. Walter was asked to become director of development for the Texas Scottish Rite Hospital for Children in Dallas. His management skills stabilized the financial structure of the hospital, and under his leadership the hospital constructed a new facility and enjoyed some of its most successful years.

When he and his wife retired in Arkansas, there was one more "yes." He ended up being in charge of a church building committee at the time that the congregation needed strong, capable leadership to help build a new facility. Each new opportunity and setback revealed another opportunity for Walter to be used by God. This was Kingdom work. God's "yes" to Walter was always connected to God's "yes" of the gospel to the world. There was always a bigger Kingdom "yes" within the more mundane, down-to-earth "yes."

Walter Mays was just a guy. That's the point. When you find your "yes" and it aligns with the greater "yes" of God to his world, things bigger than you always happen.

In the early days of the gospel, people saw miracles done by John and the other disciples. Many of the onlookers wanted to learn the magic that Peter and John had. In other words, they wanted to have the results of a relationship with Jesus Christ without actually having the relationship. But Christ does not dispense gifts or miracles for people's amusement or at their bidding. The power in Christianity is found in an individual believer living in the power of Christ's resurrection. Individual believers then use the gifts God gave them, just as other members of the body of Christ are doing the same. The magic that everybody looks for is found in a relationship with the Risen Christ—a relationship that transforms who you are into who you were created to be. There is no formula. It's in the relationship with Jesus.

You are unlike anything else in creation. Why would your Creator's "yes" to you not recognize and celebrate your uniqueness? No one else can live your life or your "yes." God spoke it into you when he created you. And it is his voice that awakens it in you today.

Finding "Yes" in It All

Why "yes" is the most important word God says to you

What, then, shall we say in response to these things?
If God is for us, who can be against us?

—PAUL (ROMANS 8:31)

have always wanted to be a writer. I have scribbled ideas on napkins and on the backs of envelopes. I have sipped gallons of coffee while swapping ideas with friends about books that needed to be written...and even discussed when we would write them. Yet, for whatever reason, I have not written the way I wanted to. There was the occasional sermon submitted for publication in an anthology, random magazine articles, and pastors' columns in local newspapers but not the books I had dreamed about writing.

Then a writer friend suggested I meet his agent. He gave me Mark Sweeney's name, and I realized I already knew Mark. He and his wife attended my church when they lived in Nashville. A couple of phone calls and one quick trip to meet with Mark and the idea for this book was crafted, pitched, and sold. I was a writer. I had a book contract and a deadline. Even better, I had an idea that needed to be made available to people. I knew I needed to get started on the writing, so I laid out a schedule in January for the winter and spring. The book wasn't due until summer. I had plenty of time.

You know what they say, "Life is what happens when you're making other plans." Well, life happened.

LIFE HAPPENS

Quite unexpectedly and much too soon, my father-in-law died. In a week's time we went from "Can you come home and help us get him to rehab?" to "How fast can you get here?" Jeannie, my wife, has two brothers. She is the only daughter. There is never a good time or a good way for a daughter to lose her dad. I don't care how old the daughter is, she is nine years old inside when her daddy gets sick and dies. My father-in-law's death was the first time my adult sons had been affected by the death of someone that close to them. I had to take care of my wife and my sons. There was no time to write. I would have to catch up later.

Later that same year I went for my annual physical. It's important to note here that my doctor is obsessive-compulsive about weight-to-height ratios and the percentage of pastors who deal with dangerous levels of LDL, HDL, and PSA. He said my PSA was high. When he told me the number, I told him that my PSA wasn't high. It was still in the normal range. That's when he pointed to my chart and said, "It's not the number I'm worried about. It's the line. Your PSA has gone up every year for the last three years. It's telling us to pay attention."

With that, I was off to see a urologist. There were tests and biopsies and a diagnosis. I had prostate cancer. After more tests and consultations, I underwent surgery in March 2011.

The cancer diagnosis and subsequent surgery did a number on me. Oh, the surgery was fine. I had no pain or complications. The surgeon was confident about the success of the procedure. My blood work has been perfect since. I am grateful for an early diagnosis and the care of skilled physicians. I have recovered well, and to the doctor's surprise, as I write this, I am almost fully recovered from the ordeal.

But I wasn't supposed to get sick. That wasn't in my plan—but there it was. And I had to deal with it. I am still trying to get my head around the fact that I had cancer and surgery and that I am now a cancer survivor. I am thankful for God's protection.

I have to tell you that one of the things that kicked me the hardest about this ordeal is the shallowness of my faith. I thought I had a deal with God: I work in his church, and in return he protects me from things like cancer. When I got the diagnosis, I couldn't fight off the feeling that God had broken our contract. Contract? It's a concept we're familiar with. When you make an offer to buy a house and your offer is accepted, you sign a contract stating you will follow through and make the purchase. But what about our dealings with God? I can't say I've seen the word *contract* used in the Bible.

Did I have a contract with God? Was my relationship with him a carefully worded, predetermined agreement for both parties to exchange services based on defined conditions? Was that the language of my faith?

I felt that I had made a bargain with God and that he had fallen down in carrying out his end of the deal. In truth, we did have a bargain, but not the one I thought we had. Our relationship was much deeper than any contract that has ever been written. I had a solid promise from God assuring me that nothing on earth could yank me out of his hands. No matter where I was or what I was going through, nothing would keep him from getting to me. Period.

Here's what is even better: he promised he would always bring a "yes" with him to whatever situation I was in. No matter the circumstances, no matter how loud the "no" that I was dealing with, Christ would bring a "yes" that would give meaning and hope. The "no" of cancer is a trial of considerable magnitude. If you have faced it, you know what I'm saying. But God's promise is always there, and nothing on earth can make even a small dent in it.

LEARNING TO TRUST THE "YES"

This idea isn't original with me. Paul wrote to the Christians in Philippi:

> I rejoiced greatly in the Lord that at last you renewed your
> concern for me. Indeed, you were concerned, but you had no
> opportunity to show it. I am not saying this because I am in
> need, for I have learned to be content whatever the circum-
> stances. I know what it is to be in need, and I know what it is
> to have plenty. I have learned the secret of being content in any
> and every situation, whether well fed or hungry, whether living
> in plenty or in want. I can do all this through him who gives
> me strength.[1]

Paul said he had learned to be *content*? That's not a word you hear much in our culture. Yet Paul stated that he knew how to be content in any situation. He hadn't achieved this because he was closer to God than most of us are. It was a simple process of learning. He had learned to be content.

Looking at Paul's story, it's clear that contentment was not some-thing he possessed as a younger man. You can sense how impatient he must have been to accomplish his goal of putting an end to the new Christian faith. Later he exhibited the same eagerness and zeal for the cause of Christ. As he followed Christ, he learned crucial lessons and, in the later years of his ministry, was confronted with circumstances far beyond his control. Arrested and held for trial, Paul was shipped from Jerusalem to Caesarea and finally to Rome. The last record we have of him is in the final verses of Acts, when he was under house arrest. But even under the control of Roman authorities, he was preaching without any hindrances. These were the circumstances in which Paul had learned to be content.

WHAT'S THE SECRET?

Paul told the Christians of Philippi that he had learned the secret. But what was that secret? He didn't spell it out, or did he? In the first chapter of Philippians, we read:

> Now I want you to know, brothers and sisters, that what has
> happened to me has actually served to advance the gospel.
> As a result, it has become clear throughout the whole palace
> guard and to everyone else that I am in chains for Christ.
> And because of my chains, most of the brothers and sisters
> have become confident in the Lord and dare all the more to
> proclaim the gospel without fear.[2]

I have to smile every time I read that passage. I pity the poor guard who was assigned to Paul on any given day. Can you imagine the conversation that took place in the barracks as each soldier read the duty roster to find out if he had been assigned to Paul? When the soldier was identified, he must have slumped in despair at the thought of another day to be spent with this preacher. It would not have been unusual for the soldier to be chained to Paul, since he was guarding a prisoner of Rome. As soon as Paul heard the shackles snap shut, I imagine he started preaching about Jesus and what Jesus could do for the soldier at the other end of the chain.

We know Paul's pattern: he would use any opportunity to speak as a chance to preach. When on trial for his life, instead of defending himself against the charges, he preached. He even went as far as to extend an invitation to faith to King Agrippa![3] I am sure Paul's time with his guards was spent the same way. He wouldn't have tried to convince them of his innocence; he would have preached. Why do you think Paul was celebrating that he had been able to preach to the entire Praetorian Guard? Through it all, Paul saw God working.

Two Lessons

However, two things about learning how to be content strike me in the Philippians passage. Both insights relate to finding our "yes," no matter what comes along.

First, Paul remained faithful to his calling, the "yes" of his destiny. Christ had sent him to be an evangelist to the Gentiles. The Roman soldiers guarding him would have been Gentiles, so Paul preached to them. That was what Christ had told him to do, and he was doing it. There is something to be said for having the courage to keep doing what you know to do even when it's not exactly the way you thought you would be doing it.

Paul was like you or me. He had big plans for his life and ministry. In Romans 1 we read that he had wanted to preach in what is now southern Europe. I'm sure he didn't see himself spending his days preaching to one soldier at a time. But, as I said, he was called to preach to Gentiles, and that's whom he was chained to.

Sometimes we think the small opportunity in front of us isn't worth the effort, but it just may be the one thing that opens up everything else.

The second truth that stands out is this: Paul was able to see himself in the big picture of what Christ was doing in the world. In Christ, God was pulling the whole world back to himself, and Paul was part of that ministry of reconciliation.[4] He was faithful to his calling even when it had to be done one soldier at a time. It's easy for us to become so consumed in our day-to-day lives that we forget that before time existed, God was at work to reconcile the world to himself. He was working before our births, and he will be working after our deaths. Our "yes" of destiny flows from the ultimate destiny of Christ. One day every part of creation and all who live in it will be brought back under the lordship of Christ. Until then, our lives and our destinies are small but significant moments of guerrilla warfare against the spiritual powers that hold creation hostage. In us and through us, God is doing big things, even if he is doing them in small ways.

THE DIVINE YES

I was thinking about Paul's celebration of his imprisonment being used by God to advance the gospel when I came across a book by Methodist missionary E. Stanley Jones. What caught my attention was the brightly decorated cover of the small paperback and its audacious title, *The Divine Yes*. Flipping the book over to read the blurbs on the back cover, I discovered that Jones had written the book during the last fourteen months of his life, the final months between a devastating stroke, which impaired his sight, speech, hearing, and ability to walk, and his death.

As I thumbed through its pages, I read about when Jones realized the seriousness of his condition. He told his daughter that he could not die until he had finished one more book, *The Divine Yes*.[5] Laboring to learn to walk and talk again, and dictating the book short bits at a time, he completed the manuscript just before his death. The stroke itself became the setting of the book. Jones was learning that even when life was shouting, "No!" Jesus was still "yes." In the opening chapter Jones admitted to his fear that he might fail in his effort to finish the book. But then he noted, Christ had used failure before to advance the gospel. If Jones could no longer preach sermons, then he would *be* one.[6]

What makes this book even more fascinating than the life situation of its writing is the message Jones was so eager to deliver: "Jesus is the Yes—the Divine Yes!"[7] Jones had spent his career as a missionary in India, at the crossroads of three major world religions—Christianity, Buddhism, and Hinduism. What he found in his discussions with leaders of the other world religions was that Jesus offered something unique, a Divine Yes to life. After the stroke hit, he was determined to get this one message out. From his own life, from all the sermons he had preached, this was the message he wanted to get across: Jesus is the "Yes" of God.

JESUS, THE "YES" OF GOD

That's what I have been trying to say, however clumsily, in this book. Jesus is the Divine Yes of God. The gospel is God's Divine Yes to us through his Son, Jesus Christ. Sure, God does say "no" to us. There are things we are told not to do. But his "no" always is couched in his Divine Yes to us. If God tells us "no," then his "yes" has promoted the "no."

Here is an example that goes to the heart of this idea. There is no more divisive issue in the political world than abortion. Just seeing the word in print makes most of us prepare to do verbal battle, defending our positions. I believe in the sanctity of life. I know there are cases where the mother's well-being is an issue, but overall these cases make up a very small percentage of the abortions in our nation. Most are used for post-conception birth control. I am sure you have heard speeches about the rights women have to choose what happens to their bodies. I know you have heard sermons explaining why abortion is wrong. With all the passionate debates on this issue, where can we find the "yes" of God?

I believe God loves the baby. I believe God loves the mother. I believe God loves the father, whether or not he sticks around. I believe the church must be the gospel, the Divine Yes to those who are dealing with this life-or-death issue. That's why, when I came to my current church, I led the congregation to get involved with Hope Clinic for Women of Nashville. Hope Clinic offers a full range of services to the entire family involved in this crisis. Remember, one of the reasons Jesus is the Divine Yes is that he offers people a way out. So the people of Jesus have to find a way to be the "yes" of Christ to our wounded world. We have to offer a way out. We have to find a way to say to the baby, the mother, the father, and anyone else dealing with this issue that "Jesus always finds a way to say 'yes.'" We have to find a way to *be* "yes" to those who are struggling with this issue.

But, sadly, that message rarely gets preached. All we talk about is the "no." God said, "Don't do this!" To a woman who is in crisis, pregnant with a baby she feels she can't support, abandoned by a man she thought loved her, despairing at the situation she is in, hearing a message of "no" might help push her into a decision she will likely regret later.

So why do Christians keep emphasizing what they oppose, making their calling card what they are against? I suspect it's because we are angry that the world isn't listening to us. We feel we have not been taken seriously, and it bothers us. We have told those in the world not to do something, but they do it anyway. So when they mess up, it's their fault, not ours. It's their responsibility to solve the problem.

It's true that we can't repair the damage of someone else's unwise choices, but being a "no" to them is not our calling. Just as you personally cannot sustain a Christian life defined by what you oppose, neither can the church. We can't live against the very people Jesus died to save. We have to live for them. We have to live for Jesus, for the lost, for the broken, for the wounded—for all those Jesus is trying to bring home to the Father. Jesus came to earth to seek and to save the lost.[8] What a powerful statement. The gospel is a liberating word of "yes." The church has to become a place of "yes."

THERE IS NO CHEAP "YES"

God's "yes" can be defined only by God, which means we can't turn it into a license to do whatever we want. As early as Paul's letter to the Christians living in Corinth, we see a misapplication of the meaning of grace. Since we love to sin and Jesus loves to forgive, the idea had arisen that more sin would have a positive outcome, causing God's grace to abound. Paul countered that misconception,[9] but it has not prevented preachers from talking about forgiveness without adding the necessary teaching on repentance.

Christ forgives us so we can repent of the things that distance us from God. But too many preachers offer a form of cheap forgiveness, which leads people to think they are forgiven so now they are free to continue in their old ways. The sad cycle of sin and cheap forgiveness has a way of trapping us. This isn't the gospel. This isn't the "yes" of God in Christ.

Biblical forgiveness is the first step toward full reconciliation with God in Christ, but it is only the first step. And when we stop after the first step, we never experience all that God has in store for us.

God's "yes" moves us from being forgiven to joining in service in his Kingdom. This is a taste of our being restored to our original place in the garden, in fellowship with our Creator. In Genesis 2 we are told God placed Adam in the garden so Adam could watch over it and tend it. Plants had to be watered, branches pruned, and grass mowed. As a steward, Adam was working with God to bring the garden into full bloom— to realize the full potential of the beauty of what God had created. This is an important image for us. God creates and gets things rolling and then invites us to join him in the work. Why? So we can celebrate him at the completion of it all. Isn't that what Revelation promises, a celebration of Christ bringing everything back under his rule, bringing everything back to its original purpose?[10]

THE "YES" AT WORK

This is the best part of God's "yes," and the heroes of our faith have figured it out. Mother Teresa engaged with the dying outcasts of India, and the entire world was brought to a deeper understanding of the church's responsibility to the poor and outcasts. Bill Wilson, overcoming his addiction to alcohol, worked with Samuel Shoemaker, an Episcopal priest, to develop the principles that became the Twelve Steps of Alcoholics Anonymous.[11] Now millions have found their way back to sobriety and health through AA. Francis Collins led the team that mapped the human genome, and through the process, we were able to see new potential for treating human disease. These people would seem to have very little in common on first glance, but each of them, out of his or her own encounter with Christ, was used by God to bring his "yes" to a place where "no" had been the only word that was heard before.

This is the "yes" we long for. The "yes" that God spoke to creation will not be revoked. He has been working his plan of redemption from the moment of the Fall until now. Our "yes" flows from God's "yes." In the "yes" of Christ, all things find their place and hold together. Even the creation hears God's "yes."

And Christ isn't going to let anything or anyone say "no" to his ultimate "yes." Dave Dravecky was a pitcher for the San Francisco Giants. He was good and getting better when tragedy struck. He was diagnosed with cancer. And not just any cancer but bone cancer…in his throwing arm. He underwent treatment, and against all odds he made a comeback. In the second start of his comeback on August 15, 1989, Dravecky was pitching in the sixth inning against the Expos when the unthinkable happened. Anyone who saw it will never forget it. Dravecky, on the mound, was delivering a pitch when his arm snapped. His arm eventually had to be amputated. He tells about his life after baseball in his book *When You Can't Come Back*. His life changed. He was no longer a famous ballplayer, but in some ways he was more famous than he had ever been. Now, through his speaking and writing career, Dave impacts the lives of more people than he ever did when he was playing baseball. He wrote:

> When I look back over the past four years and see all that I have learned from other people who have suffered, all I've experienced of other people's love, all God has shown me of his mercy and comfort, all of the encouragement my small measure of suffering has given others, I think: If I'd have continued on as a ball player and missed that, now *that* would have been a tragedy.[12]

That is the Divine Yes that overcomes the most daunting "no" that life can throw at us. A "yes" that brings life to the one who receives it and everyone and everything around that person. The "yes" of God, which we receive in Christ, sweeps us up in his glorious plan to make all things new. Quoting E. Stanley Jones once more:

> I found my numbed body and stunned mind taking fire with the possibility of going out of this life with Divine Yes on my lips as my last word and message: a Divine "Yes" when life was saying a human "No." That would be a contribution for tomorrow.[13]

When I began to understand the deeper truths of God's "yes" to us in Christ, I was excited and frustrated at the same time. I was excited to find that God had created me with a divine purpose. I was designed the way I was because I fit in a particular place in God's redemptive work. Once I discovered my own "yes," my entire life began to make sense in ways I had never dreamed would happen. But I was frustrated. Why hadn't someone told me about this sooner? Why didn't I see it on my own? My life would have been so much better if I had been swimming with the current of God's grace instead of against it. So when I discovered the truth of God's "yes," I wanted to tell everyone.

THE FINAL HOPE OF "YES"

Every day we are pelted with "nos." The world, including most religions, works overtime to tell us what we are not, who we are not, and what we will never be.

But Jesus tells us "yes," and his "yes" trumps everything. Now we hear it in bits and pieces, but one day we will hear it in full. Christ will pull back the sky and speak "yes" into the fabric of creation, and creation will remember the voice of its Maker. With each shout of "yes," all the "nos" spoken in our world will be pushed away until all that is left is the Divine Yes. The molecules will realign themselves into their original perfection. The winds and the seas will hear, and the wolf and lamb will lie down together. The Yes of God will be complete. Finished.

We look forward to the time when God's "yes" will echo throughout eternity, full, rich, and unchallenged. All those who heard his "yes" and embraced it will be with him, reconciled forever to the Creator who made them and the Savior who came to find them—all the while bringing his Divine Yes.

Going Deeper
with God's "Yes"

These discussion questions are designed to help you think more deeply about what it means that God's first, and most powerful, word to you is "yes." Use the questions on your own for personal reflection, or in conversation with a friend, or in discussing this book with others in a small-group setting.

This guide is divided into seven sessions, with each one focusing on a few chapters from *The Gospel of Yes*. Feel free to use the guide in a way that best addresses your interests, questions, and needs. If you are using this guide in a group setting, highlight the topics and questions that are of the greatest interest to group members. The questions are intended to prompt open discussion without putting anyone on the spot. The goal is to share your reactions, insights, and further questions as you seek to hear and follow God's "yes" in your life.

SESSION 1: INTRODUCTION, CHAPTERS 1 AND 2

Introduction: Our Desperate Need to Hear God's "Yes"

1. Mike tells a story about a time when he felt God had let him down, and he demanded that God show up to explain himself. If you have been in a similar situation, talk about what led up to it and what God did in response to your challenge.

2. Where are you now with God? Are you hearing from him? Is there an openness in your relationship so that you feel free to share with God any question or struggle and any cause for celebration?

Chapter 1: Does God Have a Favorite Word?

3. The author points out that much of Christian culture is oriented toward opposing things rather than focusing on what God is in favor of. Have you experienced this? If so, what effect did it have on you?

4. In chapter 1, Mike writes that being against things does not automatically make you more committed to the things of God: "Being against divorce doesn't make you *for* marriage. Being against poverty doesn't necessarily mean you're going to help the poor." How do you react to his statement?

5. Mike maintains that God's default setting is proactive—that God constantly takes the initiative to create solutions to our deepest needs. How do you feel about this view?

Chapter 2: The Problem of Living with "No"

6. Do you agree that God's ten "nos"—meaning the Ten Commandments—are actually a big "yes" from God? If so, how? If not, why not?

7. According to the author, the church's emphasis on "no" has influenced Christians to play it safe in the interest of not crossing a line and somehow messing up. He says living this way makes our lives smaller and results in our being less effective in serving God and people. Have you seen the effects of such an influence in your life? If so, discuss what those effects have been.

SESSION 2: CHAPTERS 3 AND 4

Chapter 3: The "Yes" of Creation

1. God chose to create the universe when he could have simply made do with a formless void. Why did God prefer something and not nothing?
2. God uses creation, among other things, to reveal himself to humanity. When has creation prompted within you a response of worship and awe toward God?
3. What do you see in nature that conveys God's "yes" most powerfully to you?

Chapter 4: God Says "Yes" a Lot

4. The author uses a quick review of history to show that God is constantly coming up with solutions to the problem of our rebellion and self-destructive tendencies. Have you experienced this on a personal level? If so, tell the story (if you feel comfortable doing so).
5. As you read Scripture, what story of God's having said "yes" to his people means the most to you? Share your reaction to that story with the group.
6. Why do you think God never gave up on his people? Why did he choose not to utter a final "No!" when any one of us would have long before given up on God's rebellious people? How have you seen God's persistence get through to you?

SESSION 3: CHAPTERS 5 AND 6

Chapter 5: The "Yes" of the Cross

1. Draw a cross on a piece of paper. Talk about two different aspects of God: his justice and his mercy. How does Jesus satisfy these parts of God's nature?

2. How did Jesus's becoming fully human express God's most important "yes" to us? How did Jesus's remaining fully God (both on earth and for eternity) express God's most powerful "yes" to us?

3. What does the brutality of the cross say about the nature of our sin? How did you first understand what Christ did for you on the cross?

Chapter 6: The "Yes" of the Resurrection

4. Paul wrote that if Jesus did not rise from the dead, our faith is "useless" and "futile," and "we are of all people most to be pitied" (1 Corinthians 15:14, 17, 19). What made Christ's resurrection real to you?

5. Because Jesus rose from the dead, he is present with us at all times through his Spirit. How have you experienced his presence with you this week?

6. The same power that raised Jesus from the dead is available to every believer today. How has this power helped you in a time of great challenge or need? How does this power help you in "small" and "ordinary" ways every day?

SESSION 4: CHAPTERS 7 AND 8

Chapter 7: The Mess Before the "Yes"

1. God cannot be distracted from his work of reconciling the world to himself. His offer of salvation in Christ is part of what he is doing to redeem all of creation. Where were you when Jesus found you?

2. The author maintains that people won't be able to start living differently until they start thinking differently. Paul told Christians to "be transformed by the renewing of [their] mind" (Romans 12:2). What are some ways that your mind has been

transformed? Give a few examples of how you now think differently about the most important things in life.

3. Confessing your sins and seeking God's forgiveness are the first steps in God's transforming process, but finding forgiveness is not the end of the road. It is a start. How has the church led people to believe that all they need to do to be followers of Christ is to pray a prayer to receive his forgiveness?

Chapter 8: The "Yes" of Forgiving Others

4. We need to ask for and accept God's forgiveness of our sins. But at the same time, we are commanded to forgive those who have hurt us, even if they refuse to admit they were in the wrong. Think about that dilemma, and discuss what about forgiveness seems unfair.

5. Peter asked Jesus if forgiving someone seven times would suffice, and Jesus answered that his followers need to forgive as many as seventy-seven times (see Matthew 18:21–22). Mike writes that Jesus was making the point that we need to forgive again and again, without keeping records or maintaining a balance sheet. What do you think about his interpretation?

6. Few people in Scripture were mistreated and abused more than Joseph. His brothers stole his robe and threw him into a pit, then sold him to slave traders. He was taken to a foreign country far from his home, where he worked as a servant. Later he was imprisoned for something he didn't do. Yet he was used by God to save Jacob (Joseph's father) and his family from a famine and, by extension, to keep the fledgling nation of Israel alive. And Joseph forgave the brothers who had attempted to destroy his life. What do you hear from God when you read Joseph's story (see Genesis 37–50)? What does his story tell you about forgiveness?

7. Whom do you need to forgive? What is God telling you about that person? (This is a question to take to God, not to be discussed with the group.)

Session 5: Chapters 9 and 10

Chapter 9: Surprised by "Yes"

1. The author states that outside influences join together in pointing us toward things that do not fit who God made us to be. Have you experienced this? If so, how did it affect you?

2. Do you know anyone who has succeeded in closely matching who they are to how they live? If so, describe this person to the group.

3. The author writes that by being in community with other believers, we find out who God made us to be. Have you asked people who are close to you to help you identify your gifts and calling—in other words, to name what you are really good at? What have you learned?

Chapter 10: The "Yes" of You

4. God created humans in his image, so we bear the likeness of God in a way that is different from the rest of creation. How do you recognize the image of God in yourself? in others?

5. The author argues that bearing the image of God gives us intrinsic value, independent of what we contribute to the world, how talented we are, and whether we are famous or unknown. How does bearing God's image give you value?

6. There are other ways to look at your value in God's eyes, and one is to consider the price he paid for you. He sacrificed his

Son to redeem you from sin. What does the cross say to you about your value as a person and about God's unfathomable love for you?

Session 6: Chapters 11 and 12

Chapter 11: The "Yes" of Destiny

1. What spiritual gifts did the Father give you? How are you using those gifts?
2. The author quotes Frederick Buechner, who wrote, "The place God calls you is the place where your deep gladness and the world's deep hunger meet."[1] What is your reaction to this quote? Have you seen this proved true in your life? If so, how?
3. If you have found the purpose God designed you for, share that with the group. How has finding and living within your purpose changed your life? Is your purpose now different from what it was in the past?

Chapter 12: The "Yes" of Authentic Relationships

4. The author describes engaged couples who have told him that they complete each other, as if finding the other was like finding a missing part of the person's self. Do you agree that another human might be able to complete you? Why or why not?
5. In what ways do you feel incomplete? What is a legitimate way to address areas where you feel you are lacking?
6. How do you find the affirmation and sense of belonging that all humans need? Have you ever noticed that you seek from other people the things that only Christ can supply? If so, what are ways to overcome that?
7. How do you fill your life with Christ so you can love others freely?

SESSION 7: CHAPTERS 13, 14, AND 15

Chapter 13: The "Yes" of Simplicity

1. Mike maintains that the US economy is based on consumer spending and that this is a big reason behind marketing campaigns to convince us we need to buy more stuff. How do you react to his observation?

2. Have you ever attempted to simplify your life by buying only what you need and resisting everything that is only a want? If so, what was the outcome?

3. How does clutter—in your home, in your work, in your life—get in the way of the life you really want?

Chapter 14: One "Yes" Does Not Fit All

4. What have you discovered that, in the entire world, is unique to you? How is Christ using your uniqueness?

5. How has your life changed as you have grown in Christ?

6. What surprises you most about your "yes" in Christ?

Chapter 15: Finding "Yes" in It All

7. Have you been tempted to assume that being a Christian should protect you from hurts and disappointments? If so, what have you found to be more true of the Christian experience?

8. Paul was in prison when he wrote his most famous words about contentment (see Philippians 4:10–13). Have you learned to be content? What do you need to learn, to change, or to practice in order to be content?

9. In what ways is God using you in the big picture of his work on earth?

NOTES

Introduction: Our Desperate Need to Hear God's "Yes"
1. See Genesis 32:24–32.
2. Garrison Keillor, *Lake Wobegon Days* (New York: Viking Penguin, 1985), 337.

Chapter 1: Does God Have a Favorite Word?
1. See Luke 19:10.
2. Romans 12:21.
3. Matthew 5:37.
4. Matthew 6:33, NKJV.
5. Philippians 3:7–9.
6. Malcolm Gladwell, *Outliers: The Story of Success* (New York: Little, Brown, 2008), 35.
7. Luke 9:24.
8. See Matthew 19:27–30.
9. I describe in another book how Kairos began, so I won't repeat the details here. You can read about the success of our congregation within a congregation in Mike Glenn, *In Real Time: Authentic Young Adult Ministry as It Happens* (Nashville, TN: B&H, 2009).
10. Colossians 3:17.

Chapter 2: The Problem of Living with "No"
1. Exodus 20:1–17, NKJV.
2. Matthew 22:37–40.
3. John 10:10.
4. Philippians 4:8.

5. Colossians 1:27.

6. Isaac Watts, "At the Cross," 1707, public domain.

7. Philippians 3:12.

8. See Matthew 25:14–30.

Chapter 3: The "Yes" of Creation

1. Michael Curie, Kyle Herring, and Candrea Thomas, "NASA's Proud Space Shuttle Program Ends with Atlantis Landing," July 21, 2011, www.nasa.gov/home/hqnews/2011/jul/HQ_11-240_ Atlantis_Lands.html.

2. Genesis 1:1–2:3, KJV.

3. See Job 39:13–18.

4. Stephen Hawking, *Scientific American,* "Quotable," July 2011, 21.

5. John C. Polkinghorne, *Quarks, Chaos and Christianity: Questions to Science and Religion* (New York: Crossroad, 2000), 50.

6. See Ian Stewart, *Why Beauty Is Truth: A History of Symmetry* (New York: Basic Books, 2007).

7. Stewart, *Why Beauty Is Truth,* xi.

Chapter 4: God Says "Yes" a Lot

1. 1 John 4:8.

2. Psalm 30:5.

3. Joel 2:13.

4. See Exodus 12:37–38.

5. See 1 Corinthians 1:26–28.

6. See Luke 22:60–62.

7. See John 21:15–17.

8. See Philemon 1:12–16.

Chapter 5: The "Yes" of the Cross

1. Romans 6:23.

2. John 15:13.

3. John 3:30.
4. 2 Timothy 1:7.
5. 1 Corinthians 6:20.
6. Isaiah 53:3, 5, NKJV.

Chapter 6: The "Yes" of the Resurrection

1. Shane Claiborne, *The Irresistible Revolution: Living as an Ordinary Radical* (Grand Rapids, MI: Zondervan, 2006), 41.
2. Mark 2:17.
3. 2 Corinthians 1:20.
4. See the full story in John 8.
5. John 6:67–68.
6. Dallas Willard, *The Divine Conspiracy: Rediscovering Our Hidden Life in God* (New York: Harper Collins, 1998), 95.
7. John 1:1.
8. John 14:7–9.
9. John 1:1.
10. Reggie McNeal, *The Present Future: Six Tough Questions for the Church* (San Francisco: Jossey-Bass, 2003), xiii.
11. See Revelation 21:5.
12. See 1 Corinthians 13:7–8, NKJV.
13. Ben Carson, *Gifted Hands: The Ben Carson Story* (Grand Rapids, MI: Zondervan, 1990), 59.
14. Carson, *Gifted Hands,* 60.
15. See Acts 4:13.
16. 1 Peter 2:3.
17. Matthew 6:10, KJV.
18. 1 Corinthians 15:13–19.
19. See Revelation 21:5.

Chapter 7: The Mess Before the "Yes"

1. William Faulkner, *Requiem for a Nun* (New York: Vintage, 2011), 73.
2. *Get Low,* directed by Aaron Schneider (New York: Sony Pictures Classics, 2010).
3. John 8:11, NKJV.
4. See Psalm 138:8.
5. Luke 15:17, KJV.
6. Romans 12:1.
7. Acts 10:15.
8. Robert MacGimsey, "Sweet Little Jesus Boy," 1934.
9. See John 6:5–11.
10. See John 4:4–26.
11. See Mark 5:1–20.
12. See Matthew 4:17.
13. Philippians 2:5. See also verses 6–11.
14. 1 Peter 2:4.

Chapter 8: The "Yes" of Forgiving Others

1. *On the Waterfront,* directed by Elia Kazan (Culver City, CA: Columbia Pictures, 1954).
2. Leslie D. Weatherhead, *The Will of God* (Nashville, TN: Abingdon, 1944).
3. See Romans 12:18.
4. Donald B. Kraybill, Steven M. Nolt, and David L. Weaver-Zercher, *Amish Grace: How Forgiveness Transcended Tragedy* (San Francisco: Jossey-Bass, 2007).
5. Luke 23:34.
6. See Genesis 37–50.
7. Genesis 50:20.
8. See 1 Corinthians 9:24–27.

9. See Ephesians 4:26–27.

10. NKJV

Chapter 9: Surprised by "Yes"

1. Graham Greene, *The Power and the Glory* (New York: Penguin Classics, 2003), 210.

2. Richard Rohr, *Falling Upward: A Spirituality for the Two Halves of Life* (San Francisco: Jossey-Bass, 2011), 97.

3. For more on Abraham and Sarah, see Genesis 12–21.

4. See Exodus 2–4.

5. See Judges 6:11–12.

6. For more on Gideon's story, see Judges 7–8.

7. For more on David's anointing as king of Israel, see 1 Samuel 16:1–13.

8. For more on Mary's story, see Luke 1:26–38.

9. See Acts 1–2.

10. See 2 Corinthians 11:16–28.

11. See Acts 9:1–19.

12. See Acts 9:20–28; 13:1–3.

13. For more on this idea, see John Trent and Gary Smalley, *The Blessing: Giving the Gift of Unconditional Love and Acceptance* (Nashville: Thomas Nelson, 1993).

14. The story of Jen Gash can be found at www.sweetsleep .org/.

15. Ephesians 2:8–9.

16. For more on the exchange between Jesus and the man in need of healing, see John 5:1–7.

17. See John 15:1–17.

18. Steve Jobs, quoted in "'You've Got to Find What You Love,' Jobs Says," *Stanford Report*, June 14, 2005, http://news.stanford.edu /news/2005/june15/jobs-061505.html.

Chapter 10: The "Yes" of You

1. You can read about that Super Bowl in Les Steckel, *One Yard Short: Turning Your Defeats into Victories* (Nashville: Thomas Nelson, 2006).
2. Henri Nouwen, *Life of the Beloved: Spiritual Living in a Secular World* (New York: Crossroad, 1992), 25.
3. See 1 John 4:8.
4. Brennan Manning, *The Ragamuffin Gospel* (Sisters, OR: Multnomah, 2005), 28.
5. Eric Clapton, *Clapton: The Autobiography* (New York: Random House, 2007), 257.
6. Revelation 2:17.
7. Barbara Ehrenreich, *Bright-Sided: How Positive Thinking Is Undermining America* (New York: Metropolitan, 2009), 8.
8. See Acts 9:15–16.
9. See Matthew 7:24–27.
10. See Genesis 1:26.
11. See 1 Corinthians 6:12.
12. See Matthew 5:37.

Chapter 11: The "Yes" of Destiny

1. Genesis 3:17–19.
2. Viktor Frankl, *Man's Search for Meaning* (New York: Simon & Schuster, 1959), 97.
3. Frankl, *Man's Search for Meaning,* 80.
4. Luke 4:17–21.
5. 2 Corinthians 5:17–18.
6. Frankl, *Man's Search for Meaning,* 109.
7. Ben Carson, *Gifted Hands: The Ben Carson Story* (Grand Rapids: Zondervan, 1990), 33.
8. Frederick Buechner, *Wishful Thinking: A Theological ABC* (New York: Harper & Row, 1973), 95.

9. Matthew 25:34–36.

10. Romans 8:19–20.

11. C. Michael Thompson, *The Congruent Life: Following the Inward Path to Fulfilling Work and Inspired Leadership* (San Francisco: Jossey-Bass, 2000), 31.

12. Thompson, *The Congruent Life,* 31.

13. Parker J. Palmer, *Let Your Life Speak: Listening for the Voice of Vocation* (San Francisco: Jossey-Bass, 2000), 4.

14. Ephesians 4:4–7.

15. Russell Conwell, *Acres of Diamonds* (Stillwell, KS: Digireads.com, 2008).

16. See Genesis 2:15.

17. Colossians 3:17.

18. "The Prayer of Saint Francis" is attributed to the thirteenth-century Saint Francis of Assisi. The prayer in its current form cannot be traced back further than 1912, when it was printed in French, in a small French magazine known as *La Clochette (The Little Bell).* It was attributed to an anonymous author, as demonstrated in 2001 by Dr. Christian Renoux.

Chapter 12: The "Yes" of Authentic Relationships

1. *Rocky,* directed by John G. Avildsen (Los Angeles: United Artists, 1976).

2. Margery Williams, *The Velveteen Rabbit* (New York: HarperCollins, 2003).

3. Matthew 22:36.

4. Mark 12:29–30; cf. Deuteronomy 6:4–5.

5. Matthew 22:39; cf. Leviticus 19:18.

6. See Revelation 10:8–10.

7. See John 13:34–35.

8. See Ephesians 4:22–6:18.

9. See Ephesians 5:22–32.

10. See Ephesians 5:22.
11. Ephesians 5:25.
12. See Ephesians 5:25.
13. See Genesis 2:15.
14. See the parable of the good Samaritan in Luke 10:30–37.

Chapter 13: The "Yes" of Simplicity

1. Andrew Ross Sorkin, *Too Big to Fail: The Inside Story of How Wall Street and Washington Fought to Save the Financial System—and Themselves* (New York: Viking, 2009), 3.
2. Sorkin, *Too Big to Fail*, 3.
3. Sorkin, *Too Big to Fail*, 4–5.
4. Michael Lewis, *The Big Short: Inside the Doomsday Machine* (New York: W. W. Norton, 2010), 27.
5. Stephanie Rosenbloom, "But Will It Make You Happy?" *New York Times*, August 8, 2010, Sunday Business, 1.
6. John C. Bogle, *Enough: True Measures of Money, Business, and Life* (Hoboken, NJ: John Wiley, 2009), 184–85.
7. See Matthew 16:26.
8. Tennessee Williams, *Cat on a Hot Tin Roof* (New York: New Directions Publishing, 1955), 91.
9. Richard A. Swenson, *Margin: Restoring Emotional, Physical, Financial, and Time Reserves to Overloaded Lives* (Colorado Springs, CO: NavPress, 2001), 110.
10. Commonly attributed to Lily Tomlin in *People,* December 26, 1977.
11. See Matthew 19:16–26.
12. Rachel Stanton, "Shane Claiborne Interview," May 2, 2007, https://rachelstanton.wordpress.com/2007/05/02 /shane-claiborne-interview/.
13. Shane Claiborne, *The Irresistible Revolution: Living as an Ordinary Radical* (Grand Rapids, MI: Zondervan, 2006), 39.

14. Claiborne, *The Irresistible Revolution*, 39.

15. Claiborne, *The Irresistible Revolution*, 89.

16. Richard Stearns, *The Hole in Our Gospel: What Does God Expect of Us? The Answer That Changed My Life and Might Just Change the World* (Nashville, TN: Thomas Nelson, 2010), 17.

17. Stearns, *Hole in Our Gospel*, 87.

18. Stearns, *Hole in Our Gospel*, 22.

19. Romans 14:23.

20. Anna Warner, "Jesus Loves Me," 1860, public domain.

Chapter 14: One "Yes" Does Not Fit All

1. Bruce Tulgan, *Not Everyone Gets a Trophy: How to Manage Generation Y* (San Francisco: Jossey-Bass, 2009), Kindle edition, location 296.

2. John 10:27.

3. See 1 Samuel 17.

4. Proverbs 22:6.

5. See Matthew 4:19; 9:9; 10:4.

6. See Matthew 16:25.

7. Joseph Wood Krutch, ed., *Walden and Other Writings by Henry David Thoreau* (New York: Bantam, 1981), 111.

8. Elias Aboujaoude, *Virtually You: The Dangerous Powers of the E-Personality* (New York: W. W. Norton, 2011), 10–11.

9. Aboujaoude, *Virtually You*, 40–41.

10. Aboujaoude, *Virtually You*, 33.

Chapter 15: Finding "Yes" in It All

1. Philippians 4:10–13.

2. Philippians 1:12–14.

3. See Acts 24–26.

4. See 2 Corinthians 5:17–20.

5. E. Stanley Jones, *The Divine Yes* (Nashville, TN: Abingdon, 1991), 7.

6. Jones, *The Divine Yes,* 27.

7. Jones, *The Divine Yes,* 13.

8. See Luke 19:10.

9. See Romans 6:1–7.

10. See Revelation 21:1–5.

11. Found at www.aa.org/.

12. Dave Dravecky, *When You Can't Come Back* (Grand Rapids, MI: Zondervan, 1992), 195.

13. Jones, *The Divine Yes,* 34.

Discussion Questions

1. Frederick Buechner, *Wishful Thinking: A Theological ABC* (New York: Harper & Row, 1973), 95.